PROFITABLE PROPERTY SECRETS

How to maximise your return on investment through property

STEVE BOLTON

RETHINK PRESS

First published in Great Britain in 2019 by
Rethink Press (www.rethinkpress.com)

© Copyright Steve Bolton

Cover image © TAW4/Adobe Stock

'Steve is a remarkable entrepreneur, leader and business partner to more than 1,000 people. His numbers tell you a lot… £40 million+ in annual revenues, £300 million+ franchise property portfolio and tens of thousands of raving fans!

What they don't show is that he's achieved all this as a kind, generous and wise philanthropist and family man, with an impeccable reputation for doing the right thing. If you get the chance to work with Steve or any of his amazing companies, jump at it.'
    — **Daniel Priestley**
       KPI, Dent Global and best-selling business author

'Steve Bolton was the first person I'd ever met to successfully franchise real estate investing.'
    — **Michael Gerber**
       Author of *The E-Myth Revisited*

'Steve is one of the leading entrepreneurs, investors and mentors in Europe. He and his team at Platinum Property Partners are the leading-edge investment experts and advisers in Europe today. Their meticulous attention to detail is obvious from the consistently high returns enjoyed by their Partners and investors. They are very experienced in helping ambitious individuals achieve their financial goals with greater ease and assurance.'
    — **Brian Tracy**
       Best-selling author and international speaker

'Steve Bolton is one of my favourite friends and partners in Europe. He has remarkable vision, integrity and drive.'

— **Jay Abraham**
The $9.4 Billion Man

'Steve Bolton is the founding father of professional let HMO property, my original mentor and someone I am very proud to call a friend.'

— **Ash Zuberi**
Founder, Easy Living Property

'Steve is one of the kindest, most supportive and most innovative business and property experts I know. His integrity and dedication to helping others is above and beyond virtually anybody else in the business. Read his book, learn everything you can from him, and then take best advantage of his endless willingness to give you a leg up!'

— **James Fraser**
Conservative Councillor, landlord and trainer for the National Landlords Association

'My path led to Steve Bolton after years of investing in property on my own, coming across all the sharks in the industry. Meeting Steve was a breath of fresh air and truly inspiring! I immediately liked his honesty and openness as well as his passion to help others succeed. He has created something that truly stands out and I very much intend to be part of that.'

— **Antoinette Cunningham**
Owner, Bold Investments and Lettings

This book is dedicated to:

*Lucy, Nathan, Charlie, Ella, Jude, Ronnie,
Lydie and Michelle Bolton for all of their trust,
love and support, in good times and bad.*

Contents

Foreword

by Kriss Akabusi

Some of you might remember me as the athlete who overtook American sprinter Antonio Pettigrew in the final lap of the 4 × 400 metre relay race to win the 1991 World Championships in Tokyo. Others might recognise me from my days presenting BBC's *Record Breakers* and Channel 4's *The Big Breakfast*. Whatever you know me for, it's unlikely to be property investing.

The reason I am honoured to be writing this foreword for Steve Bolton, one of my most trusted partners and mentors, is because we share a passion for setting our sights high, turning goals into actions and sharing the knowledge we've learned along the way with others. These passions were brought out of me at a young age. When I was in the army, it was Sergeant Mackenzie who inspired me to dream big and stop at nothing before I achieved what I set out to. I credit my athletics career to him, as well as my undying belief that the whole is greater than the sum of its parts.

The springboard that sport gave me enabled me to go on to build The Akabusi Company and Charitable Trust, and become a TV personality, successful businessman and motivational speaker. It was wearing the latter of these hats that led to me meeting Steve.

I was invited to talk at one of the Platinum Property Partners workshops. Whenever I do a job like this, I do a lot of research. I first spoke to Steve on the phone, and he did a great job of telling me about the company, its mission and its values. I felt I'd really connected with Steve, as most people do after meeting him. I was also intrigued by his passion for **partnerships and I** couldn't wait to meet him and the network of partners he'd built.

When the time came for me to give my talk, I can't tell you how inspiring the experience was. It's one thing to say you have a partnership of ethical people with aligned goals, but it's another being able to physically experience such conviction, energy and enthusiasm. I could see that everyone in the room embodied Steve's philosophy: *'Be More, Do More, Have More and Give More'*. Best practice, teamwork and leadership were clear to see.

The unique and highly profitable property investment model that Steve and his team had spent over a decade researching, refining and then systemising was extremely interesting. Coincidently, the timing of my talk meant it was the ideal moment for my interest to be piqued…

I was fifty-six at that time and I'd been through a few transitions in my life. I'd experienced great success, but while I had earned well, I was not really an investor. When the financial crisis hit in 2008, it was the first time in my adult life that I was affected by any sort of recession. All of a sudden, I realised the importance of ensuring financial stability. My businesses were jogging along, but nothing was guaranteed, and I was facing some challenges – literally 60% of my income could fall off a cliff top at any moment. Boom! The reality was that if things carried on the way they were, I could be forced to start selling assets. I wasn't bulletproof and I needed to start thinking about my future.

When I came to understand the Platinum Partners business model that Steve launched as a franchise in 2007, I recognised that by investing in knowledge, proven systems and a community of partners, I could secure my long-term financial future and create a legacy for my kids and grandchildren. Property was something that I knew. I'd had a buy-to-let and commercial investment in the past and I'd bought my own home. Those properties kept pace with inflation and even appreciated, in some cases, astronomically. What Steve was presenting to me, though, was the chance to build a property portfolio that could give me a great deal of profit from rental income, future capital growth, and beautiful and affordable homes for my happy housemates to live in. Importantly, it also meant that even if my speaking business nose-dived, I'd be OK because my property portfolio would prop me up financially.

The Platinum model has stood the test of time. It's based on a system that hundreds of partners have already successfully followed, and it is detailed in this book. I'm a big picture person, but this way of investing in property provided me with the detail, processes, procedures and people to support me. It just made sense, so much so that when I had a debrief with Steve after the conference I'd spoken at, I asked if it was possible to get involved. It was important to Steve that the integrity of the partner network was protected so we had to be right for each other. Luckily, we were, and that was the start of an amazing journey.

Joining Platinum Property Partners was a way to ensure that I will always have a six-figure income. It also provides me with diversity and ensures that I have a backup plan in place. Meeting Steve has been a key influence in my decision to invest in property. I'm proud to call him a partner, a mate, a mentor and a man who makes things happen.

Steve has written this book not just to talk about investing in property and making money; it's also about understanding yourself and the direction you want to go in. Having goals, understanding what skills and strategies you will need, and creating an effective support team. It's about helping to provide great homes for people who can't afford or don't want to buy, and doing so in a legal, ethical and honest manner.

If you're a novice investor, this book will prove an invaluable tool in educating you about the various property strategies out there and how to fast-track your success. If you're a seasoned professional, it should provide an injection of fresh ideas and motivation, backed by tried, tested and proven strategies for making substantial profits in any market. If you're not sure whether property is the right vehicle but are serious about protecting your future and the futures of generations to come, then much of the general advice in this book can be applied to your life outside of the property sphere.

I wish you the very best of success in whatever you choose to do in property, business and life. Dream big!
— Kriss Akabusi MBE
Olympian, Motivational Speaker and
Businessman

Introduction

'It was the best of times, it was the worst of times... '
— Charles Dickens

And so starts the classic novel *A Tale of Two Cities*.

How did I get to where I am today? Just like the Dickens novel, my own personal and professional journey has been punctuated with the best and the worst of times. My dad was a Lancashire miner turned professional footballer (AFC Bournemouth, Ipswich Town and Durban City), and my mum was a flamboyant French hairdresser. I grew up mainly in Bournemouth, Dorset, with a three-year interlude in Durban while my dad plied his trade scoring goals around various stadiums in South Africa.

From an early age, I was encouraged by my father to think creatively about ways to make money outside of simply getting a job – what he referred to as the 'daily grind'. I started following stocks and shares from the age of eight and writing basic computer programs to predict the outcome of horse races at the age of thirteen. I was also exposed to property investment during my formative years when my parents risked everything and purchased a run-down block of sixteen flats. I worked hard and unpaid as both a carpenter's mate and a cleaner during every school holiday from the age of eleven to help convert the flats into holiday apartments and support the family business. There was no silver spoon in my mouth and I knew what it was to do a hard day's work.

School wasn't my thing and I left at the age of sixteen with no qualifications. I did a few things, like working as a kitchen porter in a beach cafe and then a night-time shelf stacker at a local supermarket, before following my love of sports by taking an apprenticeship working in outdoor pursuits.

The end of being a wage slave

It was in 1994 that I finally stopped trading my time for money as an employee of someone else's business. The catalyst for me to start my own business was three-fold:

- Frustration with a job that was no longer satisfying, both financially and personally

- A strong desire to have more choice and freedom and 'be my own boss'

- Reading a range of books by or about people who had started their own successful businesses, providing me with ideas and inspiration

Having your own business is not without risk: figures consistently show that around nine out of ten start-up businesses fail within the first two years. Compare that with franchising, where the statistics show that 50% to 90% of businesses become successful and profitable. If only I'd known that back then.

I started my first business with a partner; our company built high and low rope courses. They are common these days thanks to the likes of Go Ape and Center Parcs, but back in the mid-1990s they were as rare as vegetarian snow tigers. But with a lot of hard work, and the right product in the right place at the right time, we experienced substantial growth over the seven years that followed. We were the European market leaders, employing sixty staff and operating in fifteen countries, and we had two of our own outdoor pursuits centres. On paper, I was a millionaire.

Life was great. My wife Lucy and I had a new baby on the way, a stunning six-bedroom house overlooking the sea, and a lifestyle that many people would envy. But it all came crashing down shortly after the terror attacks of 11 September 2001. The financial downturn that followed, combined with the outbreak of Foot-and-mouth disease, had a devastating impact on my business.

The best worst experience of my life

During what I now call the 'best worst experience of my life', I went from being a successful young entrepreneur to seeing almost all my assets vanish in fewer than three months. My bubble had well and truly burst.

Here is a summary of the key lessons that I learned as a result of being almost totally wiped out:

1. Stand on the shoulders of giants

I made the mistake the first time round of only learning from my own mistakes. A good friend of mine likes to say, 'You are going to have to pay for your education whether you like it or not, either by making expensive mistakes or by investing in learning to avoid mistakes from others who have paid the price already.' I'm passionate about creating various partnerships with mentors, coaches, other business owners and even competitors; this is one of the best ways to ensure success. Learn from giants!

2. Follow a tried, tested and proven system in business

My business partner and I didn't do this. We had an idea, worked hard and tried to create something unique. While it was highly rewarding when things were going well, our lack of a tried-and-tested system proved to be devastating when factors outside of our control went against us.

3. Build your business with underlying and appreciating assets

When we built our business, we rented the premises and offices in which we worked. The irony is that if we had bought these premises, which would have cost almost the same as we were paying in rent, then the value of the underlying properties would have given us a much better financial cushion when we hit hard times.

4. Make sure your business is both profitable and sustainable

Another major flaw in our business was that we didn't have a sustainable income stream. We would build a high-rope course, get paid for it, and then have no way of earning any more money from the same customer – a flawed strategy that made us only as good as the next deal we were able to land.

The property equivalent of having a sustainable income stream is buy-to-let. If you can buy-to-let and make a significant trading profit from each property, then this is a robust way to build a business.

I found myself early in 2002 sitting in a rented bungalow with a leaking roof (Lucy and I had to sell our home to avoid bankruptcy) with no business, a new baby and a large whiff of uncertainty in the air. But I had learned some valuable lessons and I decided that I would get back on the entrepreneurial horse with one phrase ringing in my ears:

'90% of all millionaires become so through owning real estate.'
— Andrew Carnegie

Andrew Carnegie was one of the richest people who has ever lived, so I thought it made sense to follow his lead. Within six months, I was once again earning a six-figure income from a new drop-shipping import business selling training and team-building products. More importantly, I had started to invest in property to secure the financial future of my family. I spent two years researching, attending training courses and surrounding myself with some of the best mentors in the world. This time, I knew what the Holy Grail of business was:

Sustainable and profitable business growth with an appreciating underlying asset base.

It was time to make my move.

A tried, tested and proven business model

I'd come up with a new strategy – letting out houses to young working professionals and key workers. High-quality, low-cost accommodation was the concept. In July 2004, I completed on my first house in multiple occupation (HMO) in Bournemouth. It was an achievement that would change my life.

All the so-called experts were telling me that this wasn't going to work. There were a lot of negative voices and it was a challenge. But I was determined. I was at the HMO every day, burning the midnight oil, paintbrush in hand, dealing with the electricians and the builders, showing the tenants in and out. My first son Charlie was with me some of the time, and as I was taking my first steps into property investment, he was literally taking his first steps in the garden of my HMO. Two big milestones I won't ever forget.

From then on, I knew I'd found a winning formula and this unique form of property investing was going to grow and grow. Within three years, I'd bought and owned twenty more properties – a portfolio worth £6 million. Life was once again good. I had achieved some huge goals – financial security for my family, a great income and pension, and more time to spend doing what I wanted.

But something didn't quite sit right with me. Believe it or not, I couldn't imagine taking a backseat and relaxing for the rest of my life. I'd learned that as well as having a system, a major part of a successful business was working with the right partners and sharing experiences with each other. I wanted to share what I'd learned with the right partners, and this tied in with something one of my many mentors had taught me:

As well as having financial security and your basic survival and shelter needs covered, to be truly happy, you also have to meet six other core human needs: certainty, variety, recognition, connection/love, growth and contribution.

I did what many other people in the training, coaching and mentoring business do – I hosted a weekend seminar. Two days of full-on value-packed information and learning. A business partner and I gave a no-holds-barred insight into what we were doing and shared our 'secrets' of success.

At the end of the weekend, we got great feedback. The course was a roaring success. But it soon became apparent that there was a fundamental problem.

When I started to check in with people a few months after the course to ask how they were getting on, I noticed a disturbing pattern: no one was applying what we had taught them. They'd all said the course was great, the information was practical, and the delivery style was inspirational, but they couldn't replicate our results. This troubled me greatly.

> 'How you make your money is more important than how much money you make.'
> — Gary Vaynerchuk

I spoke to my then business partner and a business consultant that we were working with at the time and shared my frustration. They didn't see the problem. We had 100 people paying £500 each for a seminar, bringing in a cool £50,000 for a weekend's work, less £10,000 venue costs and expenses, and it's a clear £40,000 gross profit. Good money by anyone's standards. But I wouldn't let it go.

I'd attended lots of courses run by paid-for coaches and mentors, and I could see that there was a fundamental problem with the wealth-creation and business opportunities industry. The uncomfortable truth was that the only people who really made any money were the people selling the courses. These courses provided 'information and inspiration', but what they lacked was actually the most important element: 'implementation'. That's fine if people don't have to spend too much money on information and inspiration, or if that's what they want to buy. But sadly, many course providers massively over-promise and under-deliver. They promote the rare-as-a-unicorn success stories and case studies time and time again, and deliberately don't mention the hundreds, thousands or tens of thousands of people who have failed to get a return on their time or money invested.

My Jerry Maguire moment

In the summer of 2006, while I was still wrestling with this dilemma, I went to the south of France on holiday with my wife Lucy and our children. There was no way in the world I wanted to run property seminars that promised the earth but delivered little beyond information and inspiration. Any good public presenter can inspire someone for a few hours or days, but studies show that fewer than 3% of people who attend these types of training courses actually go on to apply what they have learned. The feel-good factor after a training course soon wears off, and I refused to build a business that was based on 'selling hopes to dreamers'.

And then, in the middle of the night, my Jerry Maguire moment happened. Just like in the movie of the same name, a powerful idea flowed out of me in response to this simple question:

'What would happen if I created a business on the premise that 100% of the people who partnered with me and any of my companies would actually achieve their goals?'

Wow! What an exciting (and scary) concept that was. I got out of bed at 2am and wrote for hours, attempting to answer one question:

'What would you need to do to create a business where everyone was successful?'

I came up with a list of ten founding principles that have stood the test of time, and I've since applied to more than 1,000 legally binding partnerships of various types.

1. PARTNERSHIP

Work in partnership with people for the long term (at least five years), so that when the honeymoon period is over and the sh*t hits the fan, you can give each other the support that is needed.

2. TRIED, TESTED & PROVEN SYSTEMS

Create tried, tested and proven systems and profitable and sustainable business models that can be simplified and followed by lots of different people with different skills and experience. In essence, the business models need to be replicable and they would need to be able to work in different locations.

3. CHOOSE YOUR PARTNERS WISELY

It's critical to choose the right Franchise Partners who have the money, time, motivation and intelligence required to succeed.

4. FAMILY CULTURE

You would need to create a community and supportive family culture of like-minded Franchise Partners with shared values, who like and trust each other and who genuinely want each other to succeed.

5. STAND ON THE SHOULDERS OF GIANTS

You'd need a team of experienced mentors, subject matter experts and partners who are specialists in all the different aspects of the business. They would work with your Franchise Partners on a one-to-one basis in real time in the real world. The business **must not** be built using the 'guru principle' – i.e. one person who knows it all, as this creates a single point of failure and this in turn creates more risk.

6. THE BEST AND MOST TRUSTED SUPPLY PARTNERS

It would be vital to have a network of trusted supply partners who could provide first-class bespoke services and support at the lowest possible prices, without compromise. In time, unique and exclusive service products could be created due to the economies of scale and leverage possibilities from a large network.

7. PASSIONATE TEAM AND LONG-TERM COMMITMENT

The management team and staff would have to be genuinely passionate about mentoring, coaching and helping others succeed because a business of this type, by its very nature, would be one that would have to operate and exist for decades to come.

8. PROVIDE ACCELERATED AND BLENDED LEARNING SOLUTIONS

You would need to provide a wide and ever-growing range of blended and accelerated learning solutions, which would enable Franchise Partners from a diverse range of backgrounds and with different skills to turn theory into real-world results, day in, day out and as markets and industries change.

9. BE THE BEST, NOT THE BIGGEST

You would need to become the best company, not the biggest. And your focus would have to be on quality, measurable results and Partner success, not bums on seats and over-hyped marketing bulls**t.

10. MAKE A PROFIT, REINVEST AND GIVE MORE

Finally, it would be critical to have a financial and commercial model that meant the business would be able to afford to provide all of the above, still make a modest profit and be able to give back to those less fortunate.

Fig 0.1: 'The Platinum Way' – my Jerry Maguire moment!

My Jerry Maguire mission statement was complete and I was buzzing. It was one of those rare moments in life where I knew I had created or discovered a powerful truth – a ground-breaking concept that had not been done before (at least, not to my knowledge).

But there was one fatal flaw in the masterplan that brought me crashing down to earth:

'How on earth would I be able to provide this level of service and support at a price point that anyone would be able to afford?'

It was such a big problem that it resulted in me parting ways with my then business partner. I think he thought I was mad! And to be fair to him, at the time, I had no idea how I would ever be able to afford to provide this level of support to my future partners. I just knew at an instinctive level that this was what I wanted to do, and if I could pull it off, my partners and I would change lots of people's lives for the better.

It's easy to be a critic of what other people do, so rather than moaning about the cynical nature of the industry or looking for a way to justify selling false hope to dreamers, I decided to put my money where my mouth was and give it my best shot. At the very least, I owed it to myself and my prospective partners to give it a try. And the rest of the story, as the saying goes, is history.

Within the first decade, Platinum Property Partners had achieved great success.

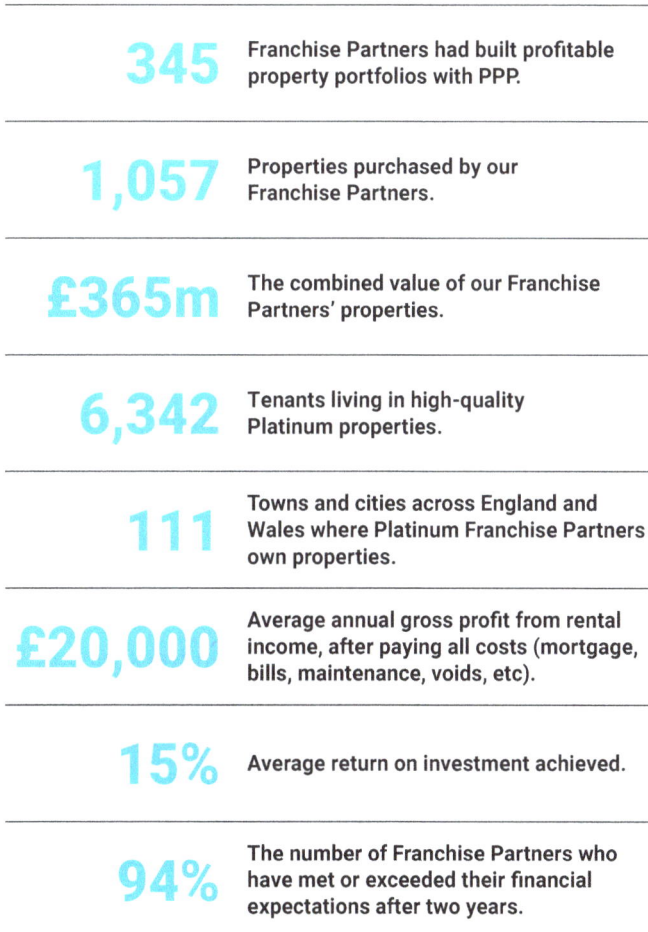

345 Franchise Partners had built profitable property portfolios with PPP.

1,057 Properties purchased by our Franchise Partners.

£365m The combined value of our Franchise Partners' properties.

6,342 Tenants living in high-quality Platinum properties.

111 Towns and cities across England and Wales where Platinum Franchise Partners own properties.

£20,000 Average annual gross profit from rental income, after paying all costs (mortgage, bills, maintenance, voids, etc).

15% Average return on investment achieved.

94% The number of Franchise Partners who have met or exceeded their financial expectations after two years.

Fig 0.2: Some of the incredible statistics that show the success of Platinum and its partners

This book lifts the lid on the critical components you need to know about this strategy, helping you avoid the most expensive and time-consuming mistakes.

Why trust what I say?

I recommend that you don't trust me because I think it's wise to have a healthy amount of scepticism when anyone is giving you advice. Question whether they're the best person to be listening to. Everyone has an opinion about property, and there's nobody quicker to advise you than a vocal friend, family member or nay-sayer. Before taking advice from anyone on anything, ask yourself what this person has done themselves, whether you admire their achievements, and whether those are similar to what you want to achieve.

If you're looking to learn about property investing from partners, what kind of partners would you want to learn from? You can't beat a proven track record, so find partners who have done what you want to do, and make sure they've had the hard knocks and overcome adversity in a diverse range of situations. It's also vital that you like and trust them, because that personal relationship is so important when you're taking big steps and making probably some of the biggest investments of your life. And don't be dazzled by paper qualifications. I'm talking about real, on-the-ground experience that can't be studied at school or university.

Has my lack of qualifications hindered my success? It's hard to say for sure, but I don't think so. By eighteen I had a job I loved, at twenty-four I was headhunted to set up an outdoor pursuits centre, and by twenty-six I had found a partner and we were launching a business that extended its operations worldwide. It wasn't easy, but because I had to rely purely on common sense, logic, trial and error and hard work, I became the businessman I am today. My decades of experience and proven success in partnerships, business, strategy, finance, marketing, sales, operations and HR across a wide variety of businesses, including both residential and commercial property, stand as my 'qualifications'.

You are never too old to learn, and it doesn't matter if you have a PhD or not a single GCSE to your name. If you want to fast-track your own success, then I'd suggest you follow a tried, tested and proven system, work with partners and people you like and trust, invest time and money in your own development, and stand on the shoulders of giants. I hope that this book will be of great assistance to your thinking and future success in property, business and life.

There are lots of books out there, written by icons of the business and property worlds, that give fantastic advice, much of which can be life-changing for those who read it – including me. I'm not trying to compete with the greats here, but from what I've heard, there's clearly a need for something that communicates the core principles of property investing as a business, particularly for the UK market. There are still too many investors continuing to make fundamental mistakes.

I've written this book to go from the macro to the micro, so it starts with the big picture before gradually getting into more detail. The world we are living in is changing dramatically and quickly, and not understanding your ultimate goal increases your risk. I see one of my main roles as reducing the risks for you as much as I can throughout this book, so please bear with me in places where you may be asking, 'What's this got to do with property investing?'

Now let's get on with the show...

PART ONE
THE BIG PICTURE

CHAPTER 1

THE END OF WEALTH CREATION AS WE KNOW IT

The world continues to change at an ever-increasing pace. Socially, hopes, beliefs and values are evolving. Where people once aspired to leave school, get a job for life, buy a house, get married and have children, more and more young people today are trying to extend their youth and live a life of travel, adventure and exploration. Marriage rates have dropped, the family meal is falling in popularity, and the typical gender roles are merging. The concept of spending decades working for the same company in the same location is no longer even a reality, as you will see as we progress through this book.

Then there's the technology revolution. The internet was young by all accounts when I was in my mid-twenties, mobile phones were literally the size of house bricks, and I couldn't fly to Geneva to go skiing with my friends for £29 return, let alone book great and affordable accommodation using Airbnb at the touch of a few buttons. The huge advances in technology have enabled vast numbers of the global population to do almost anything quickly and easily. We can make purchases online, from car insurance or gas and electricity suppliers to large household items, clothes and food, without having to traipse to the shops and spend thirty minutes queuing or hanging on the phone. And even those of us who still value traditional retail experiences are met more and more by self-service checkouts rather than cashiers. The 'Internet of things' gives billions of people access to information and learning that we could once only have dreamed of; globalisation has decreased international trade barriers; we don't have to leave our houses to earn an income; we don't even need to wait on the street for a taxi – just digitally call the closest Uber or similar.

The impact of the digital age

For many reasons, the technology revolution has made life much easier and fast-paced than it used to be, bringing with it lots of opportunity, less poverty and a better quality of life. I personally believe that it's the greatest time in human history to be alive. But, when I think of the impact of the digital age on younger generations, there are also many challenges.

If you're like me and struggle to remember your Baby Boomers from your Millennials, this might jog your memory.

NAME	TIME
Generation Z	Spans from 1996 to present day
Millennials (Generation Y)	Born late-70s to 1995
Generation X	Born early-60s to mid-70s
Baby Boomers	Born post-war to early 60s
Traditionalist	Born pre-1945

Fig 1.1: How the generations of the UK are divided up

A global study that examined the views of hundreds of graduates from the CEMS (The Global Alliance in Management Education) Masters in International Management programme found that 68% believed the rapid rate of technological and digital advancement was the biggest challenge facing twenty-first-century business leaders – ahead of political, economic and environmental concerns.[1] The 'end of jobs' perception is fast becoming a reality with job automation rates, especially in the transportation, retail, and

---

1   www.cems.org/news-media/news/press-releases/millennials-see-rapid-rate-technological-and-digital-change-biggest-c

administration and support services sectors, rising
year on year. Even those who opted for a university
education in the hope of a well-paid and secure career
are finding themselves with fewer prospects when
they do graduate, or face having to provide 24/7 communication on work-related matters.

And then there's a changing economic landscape that
younger generations have to deal with. The average
student debt is said to be £32,000 for anyone who
graduated post-2012, and that's before fees tripled.
The Institute for Fiscal Studies (IFS) predicts that three-
quarters of graduates won't pay off the full amount of
their loan, which is currently written off after thirty
years, compared with 44% of 2002 graduates who had
paid off their loan within thirteen years. It's hardly the
start in adult life that any generation needs, but it's the
current reality.

On top of this immediate financial pressure, before
they even earn an honest living, a large proportion of
young people are taking advantage of accessible un-
secured loans. Some are admittedly reckless in their
borrowing, buying a new car on finance or sticking
the dream holiday on a credit card, while others are
racking up personal debt to pay for the cost of living.

The average wage for the average person (whatever
that means these days) was £27,271 in 2017, according
to data from the Office for National Statistics (ONS).

And you'll need to get to your thirties before you can expect that. This is around a 22% improvement (adjusted for inflation) when compared with 1995, but when the cost of living in real terms is considered, my generation, Generation X, was in a much better financial position at the same age.

And as you'll probably have noticed, I haven't even touched on property prices yet. Over the same period, these have increased 298% according to the UK House Price Index.

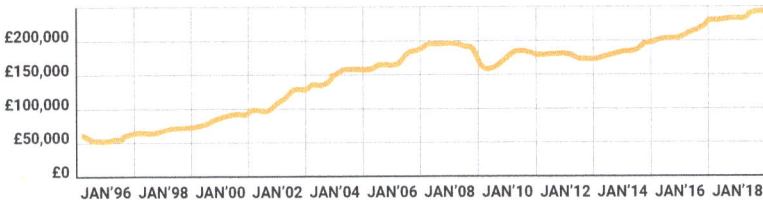

Fig 1.2: How the average price of property in the UK has risen since 1996

If you're a pessimist, here's the apparent state of play. Young people are entering the workplace with huge student debts and are being paid peanuts to do jobs they probably hadn't wanted in the first place that offer little security and no final-salary pension. They are struggling to pay their rents and buy their food while paying off personal loans and credit cards, and have almost no hope of saving for a deposit to buy their own property. Cash savings give little return and there is a constant threat of increased taxes to pay for the services that the wealthier generation are using now. It's no wonder that, for the first time in over a century, young people are likely to be financially worse off than their parents.

Or are they?

Is there a positive reality of the 'sharing economy'?

For the most part, people have created wealth from earning an income and owning property for long periods of time. This is because Baby Boomers and Generation X were brought up with the traditional philosophy that your chief aim in life should be to pay off your mortgage as soon as possible. To know that you owned your own home outright and nobody could take it from you was (and still is) a great comfort, and was often a sign of success.

As a result, many young people have been born to parents who are part of the wealthiest generation that has ever lived. And there's no nice way of saying this, but someday most Millennials and Generation Z will inherit this wealth upon the death of their parents (if they aren't already benefiting from the Bank of Mum and Dad into adulthood). Not everyone will be in this position, obviously, but the wealth that will be passed down to the younger generations will be greater than at any time in our history. Successful families take an intergenerational approach to wealth and wealth management, the older generations taking the view that they are just creating, growing and protecting their wealth for future generations.

While homeownership in their twenties might not be as easy a dream to achieve as it used to be, and therefore it won't provide the likely potential of long-term financial return, young people aren't necessarily having such a hard time of it as is commonly perceived. If I look back to when I first got on the property ladder, it wasn't all that easy. OK, so the flat I bought was only £39,500, but that was a lot of money back then compared with my £6,000 a year salary. Interest rates were at 6.5%, mortgages were hard to come by, and I needed at least a 15% deposit. Help to Buy and similar schemes hadn't even been thought of, and if I ever found myself in a position where I couldn't sell but wanted to move out, buy-to-let mortgages didn't formally exist, and neither did assured shorthold tenancies (ASTs).

Having said that, I'm not disputing that it's a challenge today for different reasons, but many Millennials, when faced with increased social and financial pressures, have shown a willingness to overcome challenges and adapt to the changing environment around them. Such resilience has spawned a culture among the younger generations which goes beyond relying on a share of their parents' wealth. Now almost anything can be shared or rented as an affordable or non-committing alternative to ownership. For example, aside from being able to share a car journey through the Lyft app or BlaBlaCar, more and more people are choosing to rent a car over buying one. Gone are the days when you buy a car and run it into the ground before you consider buying a new one. Instead, you can pay a hassle-free monthly fee that covers any servicing and faults, and if you're unhappy with the car, you can get a new one much more quickly than if you owned the car. In cities around the world, Uber has changed the game with many people choosing not to own a car at all. And in the years ahead, driverless cars, taxis, drones and delivery vehicles of all kinds will change the game even further.

Another example, albeit more obvious, is music and movies. Thanks to the likes of Spotify and Apple Music, music streaming is the new norm, and in the movie world, Netflix, Amazon Prime and other platforms are now incredibly popular.

There has also been a surge in the number of 'sharing economy' companies, which are expected to contribute a whopping £140 billion to the UK economy in the next ten years. You can now rent someone's driveway through JustPark, share people's homes using Airbnb, swap unwanted clothes via Vinted.com and exchange household items with your neighbours through Streetbank. All this is often referred to as collaborative consumption or access over ownership – where owners rent out their assets to someone who wants or needs them when they don't.

The housing market is no different. While media headlines talk of 'greedy' landlords artificially inflating house prices and Generation Rent's struggle to get on the property ladder as a direct result, the UK housing crisis has been around for decades. It is important, though, that we put the term 'housing crisis' into perspective.

In Hong Kong, for example, people are spending over £2,000 per month in rent on a 'nano apartment' which is no more than 200 square feet – about the size of two car parking spaces. The Hong Kong government estimates at least 200,000 of the city's poorest residents live in subdivided apartments. Some, known as coffin homes, are 15 square feet cages – not even half the size of a standard car parking space. These offer significantly less than the minimum 75 square feet that the Housing Authority requires for each person living in public housing. Prisoners in the city's maximum-security jails have more living space. Now that's what I call a housing crisis!

What many UK reports fail to mention is that Thatcher's Right to Buy scheme was certainly a vote winner, but it was the start of rising rents and deteriorating house building rates. Since then, consecutive governments have failed to build enough new homes. This has led to a paradigm shift from wanting and needing to own our own things to renting, and we are seeing a growing trend towards renting as a lifestyle choice, as is the case with our fellow Europeans. The likes of France and Germany do not place the same value on homeownership as we do and don't think of it 'dead money' renting. They see it as socially acceptable and more flexible than owning. As the statistics below show, the UK has the highest percentage of homeowners and the lowest percentage of private renters.

2015	Homeownership	Private Renting
Germany	51.9%	39.9%
Austria	55.7%	29.6%
Switzerland	43.4%	49.2%
Denmark	62.7%	37.3%
UK	63.5%	20%

ONS data which shows the gap between the number of renters and homeowners in the UK

The older generation of homeowners expected to own their own homes, while many of the younger generations have realised (correctly, in my opinion) that property prices simply can't increase anywhere near as much as they have done over the past thirty years. Furthermore, according to other ONS data, they are happier than their grandparents because they have less responsibility, are much less afraid of change, and are leading much healthier lives with a lot more choice and the whole world within their reach through their smartphone or low-cost travel.

This doesn't mean that no young person wants to own their own home eventually. As the sharing economy is extending beyond everyday products and services and coming into the housing market, this could pave their way to joining the property ladder. The inevitable development of longer-term tenancies than the current AST arrangement also has the potential to shift thinking about renting as a longer-term lifestyle choice.

High-quality shared living

As you will discover as we move through this book, I believe one of the best residential property investment strategies today for people looking to build a sustainable and profitable business for the future, while being part of the solution to the housing crisis, is high-quality *shared* living. Living in shared houses (known officially as houses in multiple occupation) is no longer just for students, nor are these properties the run-down squats that we all associate with drug addicts and offenders. There is a new wave of premium shared accommodation, and this way of living continues to be the first port of call for many young professionals and key workers, not just because of the affordability factor, but also because it is flexible and social.

I'll explain what HMOs are in more detail in chapter 4.

Data from the Valuation Office Agency (VOA) revealed the cost of renting a room compared to renting a one-bedroom property between April 2017 and March 2018. The 'Private Rental Market Summary Statistics' found that the cost of renting a double room in England ranged from £303 to £700 per month including London (up to £499 excluding London), depending on size and quality. That's an average of £401. The figures provided from SpareRoom.co.uk are not too dissimilar – they show that the average cost of renting a room in England was £446 including London and £432 excluding London in 2017, and £454 and £440 respectively in 2018. If we make the assumption that the majority of the rooms advertised on SpareRoom.co.uk include bills, then this could account for the increased SpareRoom.co.uk figure.

The average cost of renting a one-bedroom property, however, was £707 per month according to the same VOA report – making the cost of renting a room 43% cheaper. From experience and benefiting from a detailed insight into the premium end of the market, I know that rents can be £1,000 or more per month for a room in a shared house in certain locations, but that's also relative to the cost of a rented one-bedroom flat in those types of areas, which is much higher. When you factor in the cost of essential household bills, which is an additional £556 per month on average for food, utilities, council tax and insurance (latest available data from ONS's 2017 'Living Costs and Food Survey'), the potential saving is huge.

As you can see, renting a high-quality double room in an HMO with communal living space works out considerably cheaper than renting a one-bedroom flat, especially when most, if not all, bills are included. This allows tenants to save up more money each month without skimping on luxuries, taking them one step closer to the eventual goal of homeownership. Even for those who aren't currently thinking of purchasing their own property, it's a cost-effective and sociable way of living with likeminded people – and often enables people to live in a desirable area they would otherwise not be able to afford. For time-poor young people, location is important, and many would happily put off buying for a few years to rent in an area close to friends, work and amenities.

It's never going to be as easy as it was to purchase property and it's not just because of rising prices. The lack of available properties and people's inability to save for a deposit are the chief barriers to homeownership. But there are twenty-somethings who are on the property ladder and have purchased in locations where house prices are still affordable or have benefited from the Bank of Mum and Dad, which is the case for an estimated 25% of first-time buyers. Others who aspire to be homeowners are usually reliant on being given money, either in the form of a family inheritance or financial gift, which is the case for 30% of eighteen-to-thirty-five-year-olds according to a 2016 Aviva report.

Summary

The world has changed. I believe parents and grandparents, more than ever before, have a duty to ensure that they provide their children, grandchildren and future generations beyond them with financial support into later life. And if property ownership is going to be one of the significant challenges for younger generations, there's an opportunity to kill two birds with one stone. One of the best solutions for providing for ourselves in later life is by investing in property. And for those of us who have children, this can also be one of the best ways to help future generations as well.

In this chapter, we've covered:

- The technology revolution, which will radically disrupt the nature of how to earn a living for many in the future. Young people can no longer spend their adult lives living in the same place or working for the same employer.

- Personal debt and property prices have increased at a faster pace than wages and inflation, so young people are likely to be financially worse off than their parents. Their parents and grandparents are part of the wealthiest generation that has ever lived, for the most part because of the wealth they have amassed from property.

- Parents and grandparents have both a responsibility and an ability to financially support younger generations more than ever before.

- Rich families think about wealth on an intergenerational basis and grow and protect what they have. Everyone, irrespective of class, would be well advised to do the same.

- Shared rental accommodation suits many of the younger generations looking for affordable and flexible living, and provides a solid investment opportunity to increase wealth to pass on to the next generation.

The rest of the book will show you how you can provide for yourself and future generations by maximising your returns and minimising your risks.

CHAPTER 2

DOES IT STILL MAKE SENSE TO INVEST IN PROPERTY?

This book focuses specifically on investing in a property portfolio alongside your own home, so let me start this chapter by saying something which is probably blindingly obvious to you – if you don't already own your own home, then that will be your starting point. And, from this point of view, you would certainly be forgiven for thinking that investing in property is not the sure-fire route to financial security and a comfortable retirement it used to be. Even I have felt slightly depressed at the headlines over the past few years, despite knowing that they are only loosely based on fact and written by people who haven't a clue.

A media point of view

Before the credit crunch ball was set rolling in 2008/9, many people who had invested in property from the mid-nineties were benefiting from rapid capital growth. Some were using the fast appreciation to remortgage or sell up and use the proceeds to either reinvest in more property or subsidise their salaries and improve their lifestyles.

The majority of investors were lulled into a false sense of security, thinking of property as a quick and easy money-making machine that would generate profits effortlessly without them needing any experience or skill. Mortgage companies would lend to almost anyone, even those with tiny deposits (and sometimes more than the property value), and even if rents didn't cover the costs, it wasn't an issue. This was because the property itself was scampering up in value and would periodically give out a delicious lump-sum payment. High tide and everyone's happy.

But by the middle of 2008, emblazoned across the front pages of the newspapers and hogging the television headlines were supposed facts and figures about the number of homes being repossessed and the rate at which house prices were falling. You couldn't move for documentaries about people who'd been financially crippled by the unsound investments they'd made, especially in the new-build market. It seemed as if half the population was about to be made homeless, every buy-to-let investor had been rendered penniless, and property was the worst basket to be putting your eggs into, certainly for the foreseeable future.

The fact is that only very good or very bad news sells newspapers, which is why all we heard about was the worst-case scenario, based on sweeping generalisations. Building societies Nationwide and Halifax, along with the Land Registry, the Department for Communities and Local Government, etc, carried out research and made quotes that all sounded terribly official, so most people assumed what the media was reporting must be true. Of course, no one was making up the figures, but it's easy to be 'blinded by science'. Just because the media broadcasts and interprets an average figure, that doesn't mean it's necessarily relevant to your situation.

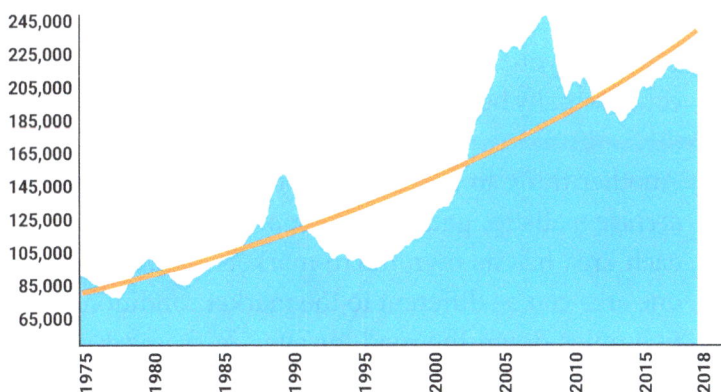

Fig 2.1: The reality of house prices in the UK

For example, when the average house price in the UK is going down, the media usually focuses on it being a terrible thing that your home is no longer worth as much as it was last month. But if the market falls by 10% and you're looking to move up the property ladder, although your home is worth 10% less than it was, so is the one you're looking to buy.

	Worth last month	Worth today, at 10% less	Reduction
Your Home	£230,000	£207,000	£23,000
Your prospective home	£280,000	£252,000	£28,000

Fig 2.2: How you can still be better off in a falling market

You may make a loss of £23,000, but if you're strict on your percentages and the relative offers you make, it could cost you £28,000 less to move up the ladder – ie you could actually be £5,000 better off from this perspective.

Another thing to bear in mind when you hear about *average* statistics gathered from across the UK is that each area has its own micro-markets. What's true in one area can be different to the market conditions just five miles down the road, or even in the next street. You need to concentrate on what's happening around your front door or the area in which you plan to invest.

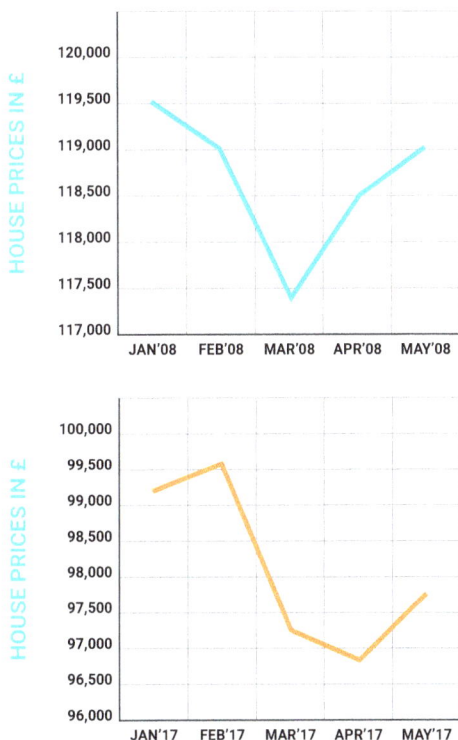

Fig 2.3: Average house price for Durham – 2008 and 2017

Be aware of the general market trends, but don't assume the headlines relate directly to you. In the second half of 2008, house prices fell in nearly every county council area or borough, but between January and May it had been a different story. The graphs on these pages use information from the Land Registry website and chart the rise and fall of house prices each month in five separate council regions over the same period of time. Alongside these, you can see the differences for January 2017 to May 2017. One quick glance is enough to see the vast differences between the regions in most months.

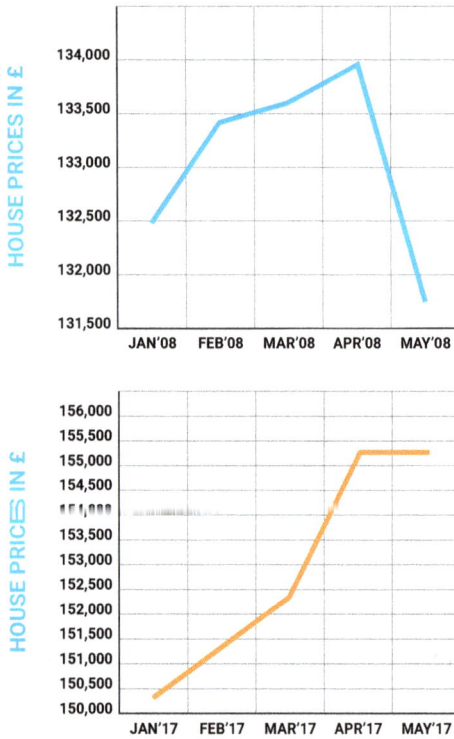

Fig 2.4: Average house price for Leicester – 2008 and 2017

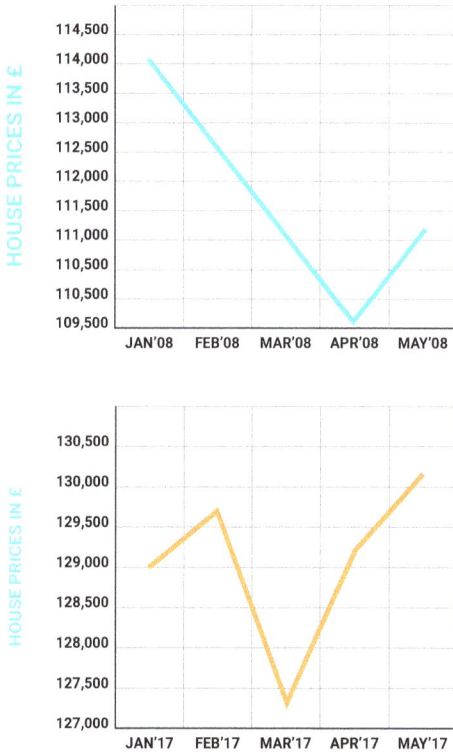

Fig 2.5: Average house price for Nottingham – 2008 and 2017

County Durham and Nottingham started to experience similar declines towards March and April, followed by sharp rises, with County Durham almost regaining its position from January. The picture for Leicester was almost the opposite, with consistent house price rises and then a sharp decline.

Just nine years later, and similar patterns are clear. Prices are generally higher, but look at County Durham and you'll see values are some £20,000 under their 2008 peak – evidence that not all areas have recovered. In Leicester, prices rose steadily at first then slowed in May, while Nottingham experienced a slight rise, severe decline, and then a sharp increase.

Look next at the graphs for Bournemouth and Poole, which geographically are right next to each other.

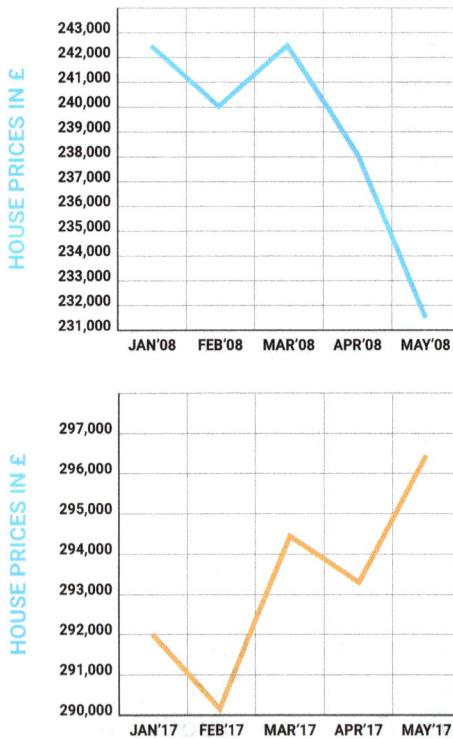

Fig 2.6: Average house price for Poole – 2008 and 2017

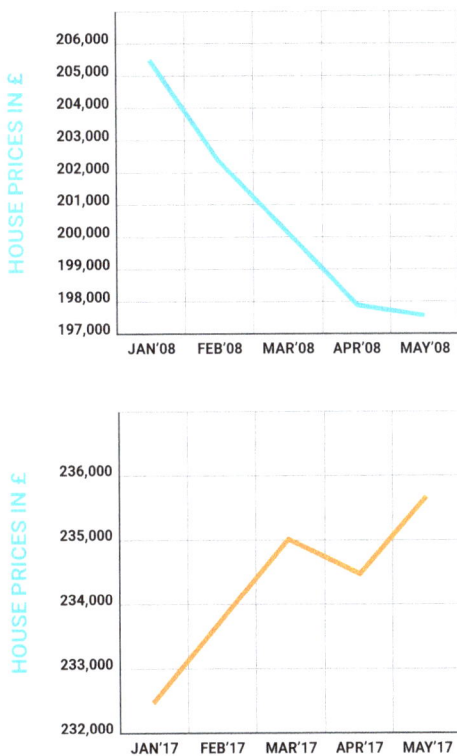

Fig 2.7: Average house price for Bournemouth – 2008 and 2017

Although the starting and ending positions on the graphs are more or less the same for the period in 2008, between February and March, house prices in the two towns moved in opposite directions. The picture in 2017 is similar, with more volatility in Poole.

Fast forward a few years, and there's a rare burst of posi-tivity in the news that tells the nation that house prices are recovering. While that was the case in some areas, especially London and the South-East, other regions hadn't even reached pre-crisis levels by 2017, as I've al-ready highlighted with the County Durham example.

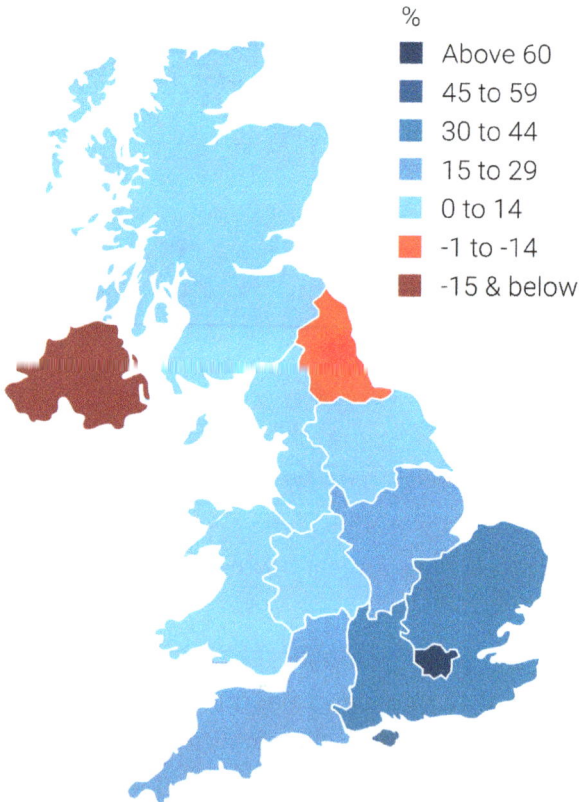

%
- Above 60
- 45 to 59
- 30 to 44
- 15 to 29
- 0 to 14
- -1 to -14
- -15 & below

Fig 2.8: How house prices have grown (or fallen) by region since 2007

You simply can't apply average statistics to your own situation at any one time; you need to research and become an expert on the market in your chosen investment area/s. 'Headline' national and regional statistics cover the full range of housing stock, so also be prepared to do some research for your chosen investment area into the specific type of property you're looking to invest in. The sale and rental values for two-bedroom flats will fluctuate in a different way to the values of four-bedroom houses – flats could be dropping in value while that of large detached houses further along the same road might be stable or even rising, and the percentage changes in values may vary as well. There really are markets within markets, so make sure you become an expert in your own investment area.

As if boom and bust isn't enough to contemplate...

Those speculative investors who had rushed into investments without doing their due diligence or paying enough attention to their return on capital and exit strategies found themselves in a lot of trouble back in 2008. It was a terrible situation for them, and not one to be taken lightly, but it was probably a good wake-up call for the investment market as a whole. The population at large became more aware of the potential downsides of investing impulsively and relying on capital growth.

But 2015 and 2016 brought even more challenges and scaremongering headlines for property investors who found themselves under a series of direct attacks. The government blamed them for rising house prices and a shortage of homes for first-time buyers (even though successive governments had failed to build more homes). It started with an announcement in the 2015 Summer Budget that individual private landlords would be restricted from deducting the cost of their mortgage interest as an allowable operating expense before paying tax. This meant that most landlords would pay 20% extra tax, despite them not earning an extra penny of income.

In my opinion, it was absolutely ludicrous – a bad tax policy that would only increase rents for tenants, reduce the supply of rental properties and do nothing to increase housing stock for first-time buyers. It didn't necessarily have such a damaging impact on professional investors because they either quickly adapted their business models or were already buying via a limited company, so they weren't affected by this ridiculous tax. However, some 1.5 million landlords have been hit.

When I was approached by a good friend of mine and fellow landlord, Chris Cooper, I decided to give him my full support in launching a Judicial Review and media campaign to fight against this all-out attack on landlords by then Chancellor, George Osborne. This wasn't just campaigning and raising awareness, but taking the government and Her Majesty's Revenue and Customs (HMRC) to the highest court in the land via a Judicial Review against the change – officially Section 24 of the Finance (no. 2) Act 2015. Our argument was that the restriction on landlords' ability to deduct finance costs as a business expense may constitute an unlawful grant of state aid to corporate landlords and owners of commercially let holiday homes, and may also breach the European Convention on Human Rights. We successfully raised over £200,000, breaking two legal crowd-funding records, and took the government all the way to the High Court. The political irony of Cherie Booth QC, the wife of Tony Blair, former Labour Prime Minister, legally challenging a Conservative government in the High Court over a policy that would negatively impact landlords, who by all accounts are traditionally Conservative voters, was not lost on the media.

Steve (right), with Chris Cooper and Cherie Booth QC

Unfortunately, the battle with the government ended in the Judicial Review being thwarted in the High Court, but with the judge openly stating that this policy raised serious social, political and economic issues. Damn right it did!

Chris and I then went on to form the first ever coalition in the private rented sector, bringing together all major landlord and letting agent associations, and we continue to fight what we call the 'Tenant Tax'.

Axe the Tenant Tax

The campaign was covered by the BBC, ITV, SKY and in all major national newspapers. I personally met with the Housing Minister, spent fifteen minutes with the Chancellor, and was propelled to the highest levels of communication within government for a short time. At the time of writing, we may have lost the battle, but we're still hoping to win the war.

While all of this was going on, an additional 3% surcharge on stamp duty was introduced for second homes and residential investment properties, adding thousands of pounds to purchase costs, and buy-to-let lending criteria were tightened, meaning that rents had to be 145% of any mortgage cost. No wonder small landlords were running for the hills. Low-yielding properties could be loss-making by 2020, especially if record-low interest rates were to rise, and it was becoming increasingly difficult and expensive to buy rental properties. Towards the end of 2016, the Residential Landlords Association reported that a quarter of landlords were already selling up or planning to as a result of extra taxes being levied on the private rented sector.

If that wasn't enough to deter many investors, a cloud of uncertainty suddenly blanketed the nation and it appeared everything had come to a halt with the Brexit vote. Homeowners and investors alike pictured plummeting house prices and soaring interest rates. Landlords were left thinking that any tenants from overseas would flee the country and they'd have empty properties that they couldn't sell. But actually, none of this materialised. Property prices continued to grow steadily, and tenant demand remained strong. While there will inevitably be ups and downs, it's hard to argue with the law of low supply and increasing demand, and that's the structural foundation of the UK property market.

As the philosopher Heraclitus says, 'The only constant in life is change'. Any business in any market will be subject to external changes, and the property market will always experience ups and downs. And, over any medium- to long-term period, it has always recovered. The result of the referendum only highlighted that investors should follow a robust strategy.

The only bad time to buy property is later

The boom-and-bust cycle is something that, historically, has always happened in the property market, and as with any sector, there will be changes to face and challenges to overcome that are completely out of your control. So long as you are following the right strategy that can weather the storms and have planned for the worst, there is never a bad time to invest in property. And here's why.

In 2001, I was in America, listening to two successful property investors called Robert G. Allen and Glen Purdy. They made a statement that had a really big impact on me.

'90% of the world's wealth is either made from or held in property.'

I researched this statistic (because I don't believe everything I read, see or hear) and found that it had solid roots. Andrew Carnegie, a billionaire industrialist and the world's richest man over 100 years ago, said something similar.

That makes it simple for me. If you're going to choose a field on which to play the game of business and make money, then pick one that is proven to have created a huge amount of wealth. History is certainly no guarantee of the future, but just look at where the wealthy are continuing to hedge their bets for long-term security.

It's not surprising given that property, and in particular buy-to-let, has outperformed all other mainstream investments over the past couple of decades (and probably beyond that). To celebrate eighteen years of buy-to-let mortgages, a study was carried out in 2014 that showed how £1,000 invested in property in the final three months of 1996 would be worth £13,048 in 2013.[2] That's more than four times what the same amount invested in equities would be worth. It's much lower risk too, but not just because capital appreciation is a given over time. This is not the fundamental and most robust reason why property can be the perfect key to financial independence, as this book will explain.

---

2   Study by former economist Rob Thomas: www.telegraph.co.uk/finance/ personalfinance/investing/buy-to-let/10788736/Buy-to-let-returns-top-allother-asset-classes.html

There are three reasons why property is a safe, secure and low-risk investment:

1. We live in the most densely populated country in Europe, but successive governments are not building enough homes for people to live in, and haven't been for decades

2. In the next ten years, the ONS forecasts an additional five million people will be living in the UK

3. Housing is a basic human need, not a luxury or discretionary purchase

On the other hand, investing in shares can be a high-risk strategy. One day, the value of your investment can rise exponentially, but then plummet almost immediately depending on company performance and economic sentiment.

Aside from investments, most people's primary source of income (PSI) is from their job or business, but this concept of trading your time for money is not as low risk as many perceive. You're only ever as good as your last pay cheque, you're at risk of redundancy when companies downsize or restructure or face problems, and you have limited control. I believe that building a property business is by far the best alternative, or addition, to other investments and an income from a traditional job or business. Around 95% of business owners earn less than £50k per annum. They work an average of twelve hours a day, six days a week, and they earn less than they would get if they were employed and on a salary. I'm sure that's not what they set out to do, but then nothing is as easy as it seems.

Investing in property can be the best way of stacking these damning odds in your favour. You can then have a business, an income, long-term security, appreciating assets, a legacy for your loved ones, and most importantly, the freedom to enjoy all of it. It doesn't mean you can't or shouldn't have a job or make other investments, but having a property business running alongside other interests can protect your downside.

It's not a game for amateurs

It frustrates me when I'm talking to people who have started investing in property and made some really basic errors that have cost them a huge amount of time and money – bad decisions that they can't reverse. Sometimes these people have bought and sold a few of their own homes and think that's more or less all there is to property investing, so they've leapt in blindly. Other times, I meet people who have been investing for a number of years and consider themselves experienced, but have actually made money more through luck and a rising market than because of any particular strategy or business plan, so when the going gets tough, they flounder.

Increasingly, I come across investors with portfolios that barely break even, and many are only surviving due to low interest rates, which cannot and will not go on forever. That leaves them stuck with a portfolio that's not doing what they thought it would, leaving them personally on shaky financial ground. It's an awful situation for anyone to find themselves in. I understand, because I've been in that very position where overlooking some fundamental business principles left me on the verge of bankruptcy.

Property is a superb wealth-creation vehicle, and if you can just get a heads-up on how to overcome some of the challenges that trip up so many people, you're giving yourself a much better chance of success. Gone are the days when any old Tom, Dick or Harry could make a serious profit from investing in property. It's no longer a case of buying low and selling high or relying on capital growth and hoping a property washes its face in the meantime. Professional portfolio investors have been and still are running successful and profitable property businesses because they have the right strategy, support and approach, whether it's a sideline designed to boost their pension, an investment for their children, or their main source of income. They're successful because they take it seriously, and if you do the same, it could be a sure-fire route to financial security for you and your family.

It's important to understand that professional investing is a different proposition to the residential housing market, where people are buying and selling their own homes. While the media might be crying out about it being a terrible time to buy, the truth is that there is no bad time to buy investment properties, provided you know what you're doing, employ a strategy that is not just for the 'here and now', and take the best advice.

While there are many ways to make money from property, I'm a firm believer in having long-term investments that are highly cash-flow positive as a solid foundation to a professional investor's business. This book gives you an overview of the common property investment strategies while focusing on one particular high-yielding model that could provide older investors with a solid and profitable business and young people with an affordable renting solution.

Summary

In this chapter, we've covered:

- Don't believe what you read, hear or see in the media about investing. Remember, when it comes to statistics, there are different property markets in each area, even each road. Concentrate on the areas you want to invest in and the types of properties you want to buy.

- Although timeframes vary and the past will never be a totally accurate prediction for the future, boom and bust in property has historically happened every fifteen to twenty years, so expect challenges and plan for them.

- 90% of the world's wealth is either made from or held in property.

- Follow a proven and robust strategy to minimise risks and maximise returns.

- Property investment can be the best alternative to other investments or a traditional job, and can give you profitable and sustainable business growth with an appreciating asset base.

- Be professional. Employ a strategy that is not just for the here and now, and take the best advice from those who have achieved what you want to achieve.

CHAPTER 3

STARTING OUT IN PROPERTY INVESTMENT

Property is not for everyone for many different reasons. There are a lot of variables to consider, so you need to have a thorough reality check before setting off on this journey.

Before you start

It may sound obvious, but the first thing you need to do is decide exactly *why* you want to get into property investing. Too many people dive into it because they know property makes sense as an investment, but they don't spend enough time thinking about what they actually want to get out of it or have clear enough timescales. When I hear people complaining that an investment hasn't done for them what they had hoped it would, it's often fundamentally because their expectations were either misaligned, unrealistic or, in most cases, not defined properly.

Spend some time thinking about your objectives, goals and desires. When you're going on any kind of journey (which investing in property is), either starting a new business or accelerating a business you've already got, you need to work out what your destination is, have some clear written objectives and apply a timeframe to them. And your objectives should be driven by what you want to achieve personally. I would say that the key driver for the thousands of people I've met and worked with is a combination of security and freedom.

I wasn't a great employee towards the end of my relatively short employed life because I value my freedom, I like variety, and I don't like being told what to do. I wanted my own business that would give me the level of income I needed to live the life I wanted, which didn't mean working eighty hours a week and having no time to enjoy the things I liked doing most, like travelling with my family, boating, fishing or improving my wellbeing. Property ticked all of the boxes for me.

For you, the main focus could be on supplementing or replacing your income from a job, building a nest egg for your children or boosting your pension provision.

Maybe you just want to increase the wealth you already have to create more freedom, security and choice in your life. It could be a combination of these drivers and they may change as you move forward, but being clear on your goals is important as it will determine which property investment strategy to follow. We will look at the more common strategies in Chapter 4. And whatever strategy that is, be realistic – you're not going to become a multi-millionaire property investor in just a few months from a standing start. Property isn't a 'get rich quick' business; it's a 'get *very* rich over time' business, so plan for the medium to long term if you're serious about creating something meaningful and sustainable.

Write down your goals, being specific about the next twelve months, have some idea about where you want to be in five and ten years' time, and review them regularly. If you're sceptical about the usefulness or effectiveness of writing down your plans, just search the internet for habits of successful people and you will see that goal setting is a common theme. I know from my own experience and that of people I have worked with that those who are clear on their goals, have them committed to paper and review them regularly achieve greater success more quickly than those who don't.

I was fortunate in the mid-1990s to work with Adrian Moorhouse, the British Olympic gold medal-winning swimmer. Adrian had retired from swimming and had started a management consultancy called Lane4, which he still has today. I was mentoring him in the world of management development at the time and we were running outdoor management programmes together for the accountancy firm KPMG.

One evening I asked Adrian what he believed were the most important things that had led to his Olympic gold medal achievement. On top of the usual stuff – extreme dedication, parental support, natural ability, etc – he also had 'visualisation' in his top five, and I was surprised.

He went on to tell me that he had swum the Olympic race in his head literally thousands of times before the competition. He added that the way in which he won it was exactly how he had visualised it and he believed it was a critical success factor, not just in sport but in business as well.

Muhammad Ali, the legendary boxer, used to call visualisation 'future history'. Ali was also an avid goal setter and visualiser. When he was quizzed by reporters after a rare defeat in the boxing ring, Ali stated that the reason he'd lost was because the other boxer's 'future history' was stronger than his.

Personally, I find making vision boards works best for focusing on my end goals. I put images of the things

I'm aiming for, or images that represent my goals, together on a sheet of paper and stick it somewhere I'll keep looking at it – above my cross-trainer and in my bathroom work best for me. If you're a parent, you can also have fun with your children.

My son, Charlie, made a vision board when he was five. The largest image of a particularly attractive female in her underwear was hardly appropriate for a five-year-old, but hear me out. Charlie was absolutely insistent it was included on his board, and when I asked why, he said that she was the kind of woman he'd like to marry when he was older. Put like that, I thought, *Who am I to deny my son his future wife?*

Lucy (my wife) wasn't very happy when she saw it, but five-year-olds can be very persuasive when they want something badly enough, and little Charlie got his way. He went on to get his advanced open water diving qualification as soon as he was legally able, and anything to do with water or boats is his passion. As for the scantily clad brunette – we're still waiting!

Once you have an idea of where you want to be and when, really think about what you're going to need financially to achieve those goals and live that life, because the 'how much' and 'when' will dictate the choices you make with your property investment portfolio.

Can you do what you want to do?

It's important that you're under no illusions about the amount of time you'll need to dedicate to achieving your goals, so look at how much you have available and are willing to commit. The average person in the UK spends twenty hours a week watching TV or browsing social media on their smartphone or tablet, but I don't know any entrepreneur or successful property investor who spends anywhere near that amount of time on their sofa. What time you're willing to commit will drive whether you're an active or passive investor. With just a couple of hours a week, there's no way you can be an active, hands-on investor and build a property business yourself.

My basic rule of thumb is if you can't or aren't willing to commit at least ten hours a week to property investing, then you would be better suited as a passive investor. Put your money into investments that will still deliver a good return on your capital, but require none or very little of your time. But bear in mind that the more active you are, the better your returns tend to be (as long as you make good decisions), especially in the UK market.

And make sure you place a value on your time – something that most people forget to do. It drives me crazy on TV shows like *Property Ladder* and *Grand Designs* when the presenters do the financial summaries at the end. They cover the costs, but miss out two critical factors:

- The opportunity / interest cost of the money used for deposit, refurbishment and fees

- The time invested by the so-called 'investors' doing the work

Firstly, if someone invests, say, £50,000 into a project, there is a cost related to that money. If they are borrowing it from equity, then they will incur interest on the funds, eg £50,000 borrowed for twelve months at 5% interest costs £2,500. If the money is coming from savings then there is an opportunity cost, which, depending on how else the investor would have invested the cash, would likely be the interest rate from a bank savings account (although that's not particularly encouraging of late). Professional investors always factor this into their calculations.

Secondly, these programmes never make any allowance for the investors' time. When the likes of Sarah Beeny and Kevin McCloud tell people they've made a £20,000 profit on the project over a twelve-month period, this is a loss-making venture in my eyes. If you are investing your time and money into your property business, make sure you aim to pay yourself a rate that makes sense.

For example, if you could have earned £50k in a full-time job, but instead you spent a year working full time on a property project that made £20k, then you've actually lost £30k. I know this is a simplistic example and it doesn't account for tax, the value of the learning you may have gained and future capital growth, among other things, but I'm sure you get the point.

Next, look at how much money you've got. If you have less than £100k of capital available to invest, either in equity or liquid funds, then property is a pretty tough business to get started in. You could consider using that money to buy two or three single-tenancy buy-to-let properties in areas where one- or two-bedroom flats are around the £120k mark (South Wales and Leeds, for example) by taking out 75% loan to value mortgages. In a low-interest-rate and high-rent market, you could make an OK yield, but in my opinion, you are on shaky financial ground and not adequately protected against future market risks. You can make investments with this kind of money, but in my opinion, you wouldn't build a meaningful business that would give you the return you really need to achieve those goals we talked about. At least, not without relying on some capital growth, which as I've already highlighted, is never a good idea. It would also take you a long time to get to where you want to be because remortgaging and taking money out to reinvest in new projects is not as easy as it used to be.

My guidance to anyone in that situation would be to start with another job or business opportunity that requires a much lower cash input – perhaps a franchise or business alongside a full-time job – and use the money from that to build up your capital. That's what I did when I started out. I worked from 7am to 6pm as an outdoor activity instructor, and then from 7pm to around 2am building up the ropes course business with my partner. It was a challenging but enjoyable six months, which built up my confidence and income so I could leave the day job. Even in my mid-twenties, I was focused on risk mitigation.

While it's possible for professional investors to buy property using little of their own money, that's certainly not something to consider if you're just starting out. It is possible and legal to buy property using other people's money (OPM), but it takes many years' experience, a strong team of legal and financial experts, and a proven track record to do so. It is also highly advisable to have other streams of income and capital reserves. It's so hard to get everything right in the beginning, and property can be high risk if you're putting all your eggs into one business that's new to you.

Whatever you do, please don't believe the 'no money down' or 'property millionaire' hype, because that's all it is: hype. I despise with a passion the 'get rich quick' merchants in the property game who profit from selling hope to dreamers.

The most extreme example I can give of unrealistic goals and expectations is a young lady I spoke to several years ago. She had paid £5,000 to attend a weekend property training seminar organised by a company that promised the earth, but delivered little. Having found that the theoretical training didn't work in the real world, she contacted Platinum to find out if we would send a mentor to work with her in the field and show her how professional investors operate.

One of our Partnership Directors asked what capital she had to invest and what her goals were, and she said, 'I want to own a £10 million portfolio in twelve months and I have £10,000 of starting capital.' Now, we like to encourage people to push the boundaries of what is possible, but in this case, the young lady needed to be given some direct feedback: what she was aiming for was ridiculous.

Her response was that she'd been told it was possible when she'd booked to go on the course. We asked whether that was before or after she'd made the £5,000 payment and, not surprisingly, she told us it was before. Our final piece of advice to her was to go back to the company and either ask for her money back or complain to the relevant bodies like the Advertising Standards Agency. And hire a good solicitor.

The more money you've got, the easier it is to invest in property, particularly in times of major market correction and threatening economic recession.

As an aside to building a substantial property business, I would encourage you, and any of your family, when buying your own home to choose something that you can retain ownership of when you move on. I'm not a fan of selling property if you can help it, so go for a property that could generate enough rent to cover the mortgage, and ideally much more. That means when you come to move up or down the ladder, you get a greater benefit from your investment than simply the capital appreciation the property has accrued while you've lived there. You may be able to remortgage it as a buy-to-let, pull out most of the capital to put down as a deposit on your next purchase, and be left with a property that will pay for itself and hopefully bring you some extra income every month. Then you can continue to benefit from more capital appreciation in the medium to long term on multiple properties.

Do you have what it takes?

That's the time and money questions covered; now you need to think about your personality type, which is just as important.

Gone are the days when most wealthy people become so through luck or inheritance. In fact, the majority of millionaires these days start off with nothing (myself included). What they do possess is a positive attitude and the determination to succeed and create wealth. They think differently, do things differently and embrace challenges. They have what is called the 'millionaire mentality'.

Your personality type is one of the key factors which will contribute to either your success or your failure in the property business. People who are pessimistic and analytical and don't necessarily like dealing with others will quickly find that property is not for them – or rather, they're not right for property. As we'll learn later in the book, property is very much a people business.

Having an optimistic, solution-oriented attitude is critical to your success, because you'll find there will always be obstacles in your way as you build your portfolio. It might be running short of capital, your properties could be subject to changes in licensing and regulation, or tenant and property management issues could be giving you a headache. You need to be able to focus on the bigger picture and find your way through the problems you'll face.

This runs alongside having the right attitude to risk and debt. You need to really think how you feel about getting yourself into hundreds of thousands or even millions of pounds worth of debt, because by the time you've got four or five properties, it's highly likely that's what your mortgage borrowing will have hit. If that thought terrifies you and you're not comfortable with the idea of having high loan-to-value borrowing on a property, then I'd suggest you keep reading. This book will help clarify just what property investing is all about, explaining the value of debt and how, if used correctly, it can be your friend. There is a big difference between 'good debt' and 'bad debt', which I'll clarify in Chapter 7.

Without the right attitude, you will miss opportunities, slow your progress down, and may well stall before you've started. Having worked with hundreds, if not thousands, of people on their property investment journeys over the past 30+ years, I have found that those who are successful tend to possess certain practical skills and mental attributes.

KNOWLEDGE	They have invested time and money into educating themselves about property investment, have a willingness to keep learning and feel confident in their chosen strategies.
FINANCE	They are financially astute, have strong money management skills and understand the numbers and KPIs involved in running a successful property portfolio.
TIME	They are able to effectively manage their time and prioritise the most beneficial activities.
DRIVE	They are persistent, solution-focused, action-oriented and determined to achieve success and overcome obstacles.
GOALS	They never lose sight of why they are doing it, and always review where they are and how they are going to get there.
RISK	They understand, assess and mitigate against risks from the start. Then they are willing to take carefully calculated risks and always have a Plan B, C and D.

Fig 3.1: The skills and attributes of successful people

Time and time again, people come to me or my partners who have the capital to invest in building a property portfolio, but they don't have the right attitude and mindset. It would never work for them because they don't have the motivation to change the way they do things, and sometimes, they are considering property for all the wrong reasons.

This was one of the reasons that I decided to work with an IT company and developer to build the Property Investor Profile. I use it as a way of helping people understand if property is right for them, and they are right for property. Don't get me wrong, you aren't born with the practical skills needed to be a successful investor, but you at least need to be willing to change your mindset so that you are open to developing those skills.

You can take the test here: www.propertyinvestorprofile.com

Who you are encompasses a huge variety of factors, but in terms of building a property business, the most important assets are self-confidence, time and money management, and communication skills. Property is a people business first and foremost. You need to have excellent negotiation skills, people have to like and want to work with you, and you must always do business with integrity.

Are you ready to run a business?

Property investing is a fantastic opportunity and a superb wealth-creation tool, but be under no illusion. Building and running your own property portfolio is a business, and as such, a key part of it is all about balance sheets, profit and loss, and cash flow. And for anyone looking at starting their own business, there's good and bad news.

The great news is that you're independent, you're working for yourself and not making profit to line anyone else's pocket. If you choose the right business and have a specific strategy in place, you can reach the first level of financial independence – where you don't have to trade your time for money – relatively quickly. That, in turn, gives you more choices, and if you're leveraging other people's time, money and resources properly, you'll be getting richer even while you sleep. Doing all this, with the right values and conducting your business in an ethical way, will allow you to be more, do more, have more and give more, and you'll find yourself tremendously successful and an inspiration to others.

The bad news is that the average millionaire has been bankrupt, or close to bankruptcy, three times before working out how to sustain their wealth, according to Brian Tracy (voted one of the top three motivational speakers in the world and someone I am extremely fortunate to call a mentor and friend). A tiny minority are naturally wired for success – they have the right beliefs, skills and personalities, select the right opportunities and are in the right place at the right time. It seems they can't fail – people like Michael Dell and Bill Gates, who made their first million when they were young and have never looked back. But these kinds of people – the people I like to call the unicorns in business – are very much the exception to the rule. For the vast majority, there are going to be gaps, weaknesses and blind spots in terms of the process of becoming wealthy.

Having personally been wiped out once – not bankrupt, but pretty close to it – and having had a number of successful businesses, I found out the hard way the importance of making sure you have a solid foundation of business fundamentals in place. I have a lot of respect for businesspeople and entrepreneurs who have taken the knocks, because they will have gained wisdom that goes beyond that of someone who's only ever experienced success. They tend to make better mentors because they have overcome adversity and found solutions, and they can absolutely identify with the concerns and fears of people just starting out.

I can't stress enough the importance of understanding the business fundamentals – things like cash flow, how to manage staff, how to establish and keep good tax, bookkeeping and accounting records, how to sell, how to market, etc. There are many skills involved in running a property business, so you need to make sure you're prepared for it.

Unlike the commonly held myth that there is one fixed set of traits that makes people successful, I subscribe to the belief that many different types of people can achieve success, as long as they are working in a role and a business that suits their natural strengths and talents. Around 90% of businesses fail within the first two years, and lack of adequate cash flow is the primary reason. Most people are over-optimistic. There's a good rule of thumb in business that whatever your goals are, they typically take twice as long and cost twice as much to achieve as your forecasts suggest, so one bit of advice I give people is whatever you think it's going to cost you and however long you think it's going to take, double both. The caveat to this is with experience, you can become much more confident. One of the advantages I have today, with more than 1,000 properties all over the UK through my partner network, is that I can be very confident of the returns I will make.

What's interesting – backing up the principle of mentoring and 'standing on the shoulders of giants' – is if you look at franchising, that statistic is reversed: 94% of franchises succeed and are still going two years on. Not only that, 90% of them are also profitable within the first two years.[3] So there's a strategic decision you need to make: whether to go it alone and have a high chance of failure, or buy into some kind of proven system with a much higher probability of success. I'd strongly recommend the latter.

Ultimately, success comes down to a combination of having the desire, the motivation and some burning ambition, and making sure your business and the people you work with are aligned with your values.

---

3   NatWest/bfa *Annual Franchise Report*

Every individual has a set of values, whether they're consciously aware of it or not. They are the things that fundamentally drive an individual's behaviour.

If you value variety and independence, then your chances of being successful in your own business are likely to be higher than those of someone who is quite comfortable being an employee and working for someone else who pays their wages. And if you're an employee who's been made redundant and forced into a situation where you have to consider starting your own business, then you're going to have a different approach to someone who's taken the deliberate step to become self-employed because of their values and key drivers.

Summary

In this chapter, we've covered:

- Being clear about why you're investing in property

- Having written and financial goals and set timescales

- Deciding how much time you're willing and able to commit to your property business

- Understanding that it's difficult to invest in property without a significant amount of your own capital to start with

- Having the right attitude and mentality

- Becoming comfortable with the idea of risk and debt

- Remembering that investing in property is a business

Whatever kind of person you are, creating a highly profitable property portfolio can be a long and rocky road. Whether you're just starting out or have already got a portfolio that may not be performing as well as it could, this book will give you a helping hand.

In the following chapters, I'll be highlighting some of the key mistakes investors make and looking at how you can:

- Maximise your income

- Minimise your risks

- Get the best return on your capital

- Build a balanced portfolio that will bring you high returns

- Achieve long-term financial security

- Systemise your business so you can spend more time working on it instead of in it

PART TWO
THE SEVEN MISTAKES

CHAPTER 4

MISTAKE #1 – NOT ADOPTING THE RIGHT STRATEGY

Now you have an understanding of *why* you want to invest in property, the key is to make sure you minimise the risks and maximise the odds of achieving what you have set out to achieve, which comes back to making sure you have spent time doing personal preparation and understanding your own motivation, aims and goals in the first place. Once you have an idea of what kind of investments you need to make to get the results you're looking for, you will be most effective if you follow a proven, disciplined, well-thought-out plan.

Let's detail some of the property investment strategies available to you – and there are many, so I'll stick to the most common ones.

Aside from your own home (even though, as I mentioned in the last chapter, it can be the asset that starts your journey), property investment strategies usually fall into the following categories:

- Buy-to-sell

- Residential property development

- Fly-to-let

- Buy-to-let

- HMOs

- Commercial

I'm not going to go into detail about commercial property investment because it is for sophisticated investors, so never consider starting out in this area. There are several sub-strategies within commercial in terms of the type of property (serviced offices, warehouses, hotels, retail space, etc) and objectives (planning gains, capital value, yield, yield compression, lease negotiations, permitted development, development, etc), which are not the focus of this book. All I would like to do is share some information on a commercial property project I was involved in.

CASE STUDY: BEYOND RESIDENTIAL...

In 2013, my partners and I bought a serviced office building in Bournemouth through the commercial arm of our group of companies. It was losing money because it had been neglected and was only 50% occupied. After giving the building a makeover, employing a dedicated management team, improving the services and re-letting units to small businesses, we increased the financial return by 340% in the first year alone.

As part of our asset management programme, we developed the garage space and converted it into usable office space, which generated an additional £120,000 annual income for a one-off capital outlay of £100,000. Alongside this, we applied for and won planning permission to convert the existing building into residential apartments and build an additional two floors, which gave us a planning gain. Despite this latter part of the project involving no physical changes at this time, we essentially land banked the profit from the enhanced future gross development value (GDV).

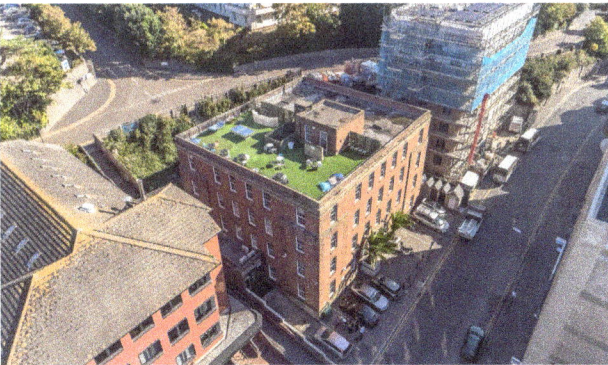

As you can probably imagine, this project took up a lot of time and hard work, and involved dealing with many moving parts, different building and planning regulations, and external parties, including local authorities, architects and investors, so it's not the type of project for the inexperienced property investor. This case study simply highlights a future development path beyond residential investment. Commercial property investment is a great strategy, but I strongly recommend you gain a lot of experience in the residential market before even considering this route.

I'll now work through the rest of the strategies I listed.

Buy-to-sell

This is the most commonly promoted strategy on TV programmes such as *Homes Under the Hammer* where investors purchase a property with the aim of reselling it for a profit. This is often referred to as 'flipping', and the specifics can vary.

At one end of the spectrum, many people do this with their own homes. They'll buy run-down properties, completely refurbish and renovate them while living in them, and sell a couple of years down the line. It's something that can work when you're starting out, and actually, it was exactly what I did with my first property.

It was a run-down two-bedroom flat in Swanage, Dorset. I bought it for £39,500 in 1992, completely renovated it and did a loft conversion with the help of my dad, and sold it two years later for £65,000. Happy days and decent money in my early twenties. Doing the work in my spare time, in the evenings and at weekends proved to be a profitable hobby. And that's why so many other people start the same way.

CASE STUDY

While working as a physiotherapist for the NHS and bringing up her three children, Platinum Property Partner, Judy Mizen, found she had a passion for property renovation. She loved doing up her own homes and moving on to the next one. For her, it gave her enough money to turn a passion into a business. She progressed to building a good portfolio of HMOs generating a substantial annual gross profit, has built her own home, and has branched out into investing in commercial property.

At the other end of the spectrum are the professional investors who aim to buy cheap properties, often lower than market value, do the work and sell as quickly as possible for as much profit as possible. Much of the time, they are relying on luck, because as good a bargain as the property might be and as good as they are at project, budget and people management, they need a stable or rising market.

> 'A rising tide floats all boats... only when the tide goes out do you discover who's been swimming naked.'
> — Warren Buffett

You can buy badly, spend too much and make huge mistakes, but if the market has gone up by 40%, then you can still make money. A critical factor to success is timing in this strategy.

People who do buy-to-sell well are good with detail, numbers and people. They don't do it just for the money; they do it because they enjoy it. I'm a great believer that you make the most money out of what you enjoy doing the most, but it's not a strategy for me. I'm not a high-detail person and I consider it to be quite a risky strategy, not just for novices, but intermediates too. Be mindful that if you consider this particular approach, you're only as good as your last deal, you're susceptible to changes in the market, and the risk profile is much higher.

Residential property development

This strategy is similar to buy-to-sell, but differs in that it's not just light refurbishment and low-level conversion, which won't usually require planning permission; it's another ball game altogether. Residential property development, whether you're building in your back garden, buying land, or flattening a property and redeveloping on the space, will definitely require planning permission.

It could involve major conversion works, both internally and externally; the construction of new properties on land; demolition of existing properties; or the redevelopment of new flats or houses. A bit like commercial, it's a much more sophisticated investment strategy than buy-to-sell, but like buy-to-sell, there are a number of factors outside your control which increase the risk profile, for example, the state of the market in terms of your ability to find buyers to purchase at the right price. There's also the added complexity of things such as management of significant building projects, planning risk and approval, building regulation sign off, and issues with regards to financing and funding projects.

Your ability to get finance from banks will very much depend on your and your team's track record on development projects, so this is really only a strategy for once you have graduated from other areas of property investing, like buy-to-sell and buy-to-let. For sure, you will need significant support from a wide range of qualified professionals and experienced individuals.

To highlight the risks involved with this strategy, I reflect back to the financial crisis of 2007/8. I had many friends who were property developers, and within twelve months, around half of them had gone out of business. Those who had personally guaranteed their projects to secure bank financing lost their homes, and in some cases, even went bankrupt.

This is not a strategy for the faint of heart or the inexperienced investor. It can be highly rewarding and profitable if you get it right, but I have seen far more people get it wrong. My focus has always been to minimise risks and maximise returns, so this is not a strategy I'll be going into in detail in the book.

Fly-to-let

This can mean sophisticated overseas investing, but here I'm going to be talking about holiday homes. Whether they're abroad or in the UK is irrelevant.

When you can combine making money with having a property in a location of your choice for exclusive use whenever you want it, what's not to like? Many years ago, I had a home on the Gulf Coast in Florida, a ski chalet in Chamonix and villa on the French Riviera on my vision board. I, like so many other people, had a romantic notion of having a holiday home… and then I did the numbers. What this proved to me was that it was a completely flawed investment strategy for most people because of the burden of ownership and the likely financial return.

If you're considering buying a holiday home, please first do this: work out the number of days you'll realistically be using the property and compare that with what it would cost to book a holiday for the same amount of time in the same area. If owning the holiday home is cheaper, that's a great start.

Now compare the actual cost of the investment – the purchase costs, finance costs if it's mortgaged, maintenance, management and leasehold fees, and the time and monetary costs of advertising and renting it out (not to mention the stress and seasonal variations and tax) – with the return you'd get from investing that money elsewhere. After looking at the income and expenditure and assuming zero capital growth (because that should be a bonus, not a strategy), you'll probably find that the financial return is negative.

If the numbers do stack up, then ask yourself if you and your family would be happy returning to the same place over and over again. If you have kids, how long before they start complaining they're bored with it? How soon will the novelty wear off? (It's after two to three years usually.)

If your family eventually wants to live in a certain location or you want to retire there, then that's different, but never think of a holiday home as an investment decision. It's a lifestyle decision.

Not everything we buy has to give back to us financially, though. Take cars, for example. We buy them, they go down in value and cost money to run, but we need them to get around, and some people get a lot of pleasure from them. If you find a place that you love and you know you're going to go back to, and the property at least washes its face, then who am I to tell you not to go for it?

One of my business partners has a property in Chamonix, but he lives in Dorset. He goes to Chamonix every other weekend, loves the mountains, does his best thinking there and it's his second home. That's an example of how it can work for someone, but I can count on the fingers of one hand the number of people I've met over the years who are totally happy with their decision to buy a holiday home in the long term – and I've met hundreds of people with holiday homes.

On a lighter note, a long-standing franchise partner, Suky Walia, a legend and one of my closest friends, has a holiday home fifteen minutes from where he lives in Newcastle. To most normal people, that concept seems absolutely bizarre, but to Suky, it makes complete sense. He says he can finish work, jump in the car, drive for fifteen minutes and feel like he's on holiday. Then there's the added benefit that if he forgets his toothbrush, he can pop back home and pick it up, and he's back on holiday thirty minutes later.

You'd have to meet Suky to understand why this seems like a completely logical decision to him!

To balance the argument, I have to admit that Suky did call me out on also having a holiday home close to where I live. I have a boat in a marina at Sandbanks in Poole harbour, which is just ten minutes from my home in Bournemouth. Suky knows that I sometimes sleep on my boat and take the family out on it a lot.

He asked me, 'What's the difference between your holiday home and mine?' I said that I can go to France or explore the south coast of England in mine. This didn't seem to matter to him, and now he takes the mickey out of me for having a 'holiday home' ten minutes from where I live.

Buy-to-let

This is probably the most well-known and widely adopted investment strategy in the UK, and it's been that way for many decades. There are millions of accidental amateur landlords – those who have rented out a property that they used to live in to supplement their income or provide a top-up to their pension. They either bought using cash, inherited the property or financed with a mortgage, and as long as the rent covered the mortgage payments, they handed everything over to a letting agent and forgot about it.

Financially, most people were happy to ensure that the property didn't make a loss, and they relied on long-term capital growth to generate any form of profit. During periods of rapidly increasing property values, minimal legislation and a good tax environment, income returns were solid and capital gain prospects were great. A lot of people made a lot of money from buying property and renting it out for a long time.

Standard buy-to-let as we know it – renting out a property on a single-occupancy basis – can and still does work in some instances, but with these caveats:

- You have to buy the right property at the right price in the right location, ideally with a discount

- You have to ensure the yield is as high as possible

- Don't have a high level of gearing (buy for cash or keep your loan to value low)

If you are comparing buy-to-let with having money sitting in a bank earning you 1% or 2% interest, then it could be a good option for you. It's a good strategy if you are cash rich, relatively unsophisticated in investment terms, and you don't aspire to be hands-on or have a big portfolio or high income. But the lack of income means you are far more susceptible to negative outcomes in the market, such as interest-rate rises or voids if you are highly geared.

The problem is that if you don't know much about property investment and go to an estate agent, they will assume single-occupancy buy-to-let is the right strategy for you. At the end of the day, you don't know what you don't know, and a lack of understanding about what's possible could mean that you make the wrong decision.

HMOs

There is a more robust buy-to-let strategy, and for reasons that will become clear, this will be the major focus of the rest of this book. The HMO model, which maximises the number of lettable rooms or units in a single property by renting them individually, vastly increases rental income, which in turn ensures better profit margins and minimises risk. To define vastly, I'm talking about 200% to 400% more rental income than single-occupancy buy-to-let. In the first ten years of trading, from 2007 to 2017, my Platinum Property Partners bought and converted more than 1,000 properties into HMOs.

I usually break the HMO strategy down into three categories:

	High Quality	
Professional	Average Quality	
Let HMO	Low Quality	
	High Quality	
Student	Average Quality	
Let HMO	Low Quality	
	High Quality	
LHA	Average Quality	
Let HMO	Low Quality	

HMOs are generally defined as properties with a minimum of three unconnected tenants (ie not related or part of the same household) sharing kitchen, bathroom and toilet facilities. The bedrooms or units will be rented individually rather than as one property, maximising the total rental income.

For some time, this model of renting out multiple rooms on an individual basis has been commonly associated with student lets, bedsits and Local Housing

Authority (LHA) benefit tenants. Typically, the view is that such properties are low standard accommodation. And HMO properties can generate excellent returns no matter the quality (although this raises several legal and ethical questions).

At the lower end of the HMO market, landlords cater specifically for housing-benefit tenants. Their properties achieve lower rents, experience higher management issues, and often capital appreciation is below average because of the areas in which they are typically located.

In the middle are student HMOs – a great strategy for people in university locations as, although they generate modest rents, there's a high demand for the properties. However, there are a number of downsides to be aware of. Student properties are often poorly maintained by the tenants, empty for a few months of the year (summer breaks), and require major refurbishments during tenancy changeovers. Student HMO landlords have also been facing stiff competition for many years from the big halls of residence providers. These blocks usually contain five- or six-bedroom flats with shared kitchen and bathroom facilities, and the operators have long-term contracts with universities, which often agree to fill them with first-year students. In many areas, halls of residence are overtaking shared houses as the accommodation of choice for students.

As far back as 2007, I was with one of my partners in Southsea (close to Portsmouth) to look at large quantities of empty student houses. They weren't selling because tenant demand had fallen through the floor.

Aside from housing-benefit and student HMOs, since the early 2000s, a different breed of HMO has emerged because the demand for affordable, high-quality shared housing has increased. These HMOs have become especially popular with graduates and young professionals who can't afford to or don't want to buy their own homes. And this is the HMO sector that makes most sense if you are serious about earning a lifelong income from property.

Intelligent, professional and adequately funded investors operate in this space because it's a model that not only generates the highest returns (200–400% more than single-tenancy and other HMO models), but also makes efficient use of housing stock and creates more homes from the same space. At the same time, it provides Generation Rent with affordable, safe and sociable homes, which are all attractive reasons for considering investment in this type of asset class.

But it's not a walk in the park. Higher returns usually come with a bigger price tag from the outset and increased time investment. As well as the time and cost involved in finding, purchasing and refurbishing appropriate properties, there are also complex planning, licensing and building regulations to consider (which are always changing), not to mention the management of multiple tenants in multiple properties. There are a lot of mistakes investors can make, so only those with the available capital and the desire and motivation to build a proper property business will succeed. But for me, and for everyone who has joined Platinum Property Partners, professional HMOs are the Holy Grail of property investment.

The Holy Grail in business

Over the past thirty years of being in business with scores of different companies and in a variety of different sectors, I have developed a five-step checklist that I call my Holy Grail. You can apply this model of thinking to any business, in any industry. I'd strongly recommend you tick as many boxes as possible when considering any investment or business venture.

For me, professional-let HMOs fulfil all five principles of my Holy Grail checklist:

1.	Profitable and sustainable business growth
2.	Underpinned by appreciating assets
3.	Structured in a highly tax-efficient manner
4.	Can be systemised and outsourced so others can operate the business for you
5.	Can be operated from anywhere in the world

In my opinion, strategy always trumps tactics in business, so ensuring that you start out with the right business strategy and investment model that can achieve your medium- to long-term lifestyle objectives is a key priority. I've met too many people in my life who take a job or start a business to earn or make money, but haven't really thought through the consequences of their strategy. As one of my past mentors, Stephen Covey, teaches, 'Begin with the end in mind'. The clearer you can be upfront about where you want to be and how your business is going to support your personal goals, the better it will be for you.

Don't make the mistake of putting the business cart before your lifestyle horse. What I mean by that is start by focusing on your personal needs, as we discussed in the previous chapter, and choose a business strategy that will support your lifestyle goals. Remember, most people spend more time planning their summer holiday than they do the rest of their life. Please don't make that mistake. Be clear on your personal and lifestyle goals and build your business around them, as opposed to the other way around.

People who know where they are going usually get there.

Your strategy checklist

The following list, when combined with the Holy Grail, will give you a good framework for your strategic direction. Ensure that:

1.	Your leveraged income exceeds your monthly expenses
2.	You have multiple streams of income
3.	You have clear exit strategy/ies in place
4.	You protect your downside

Let's look at these in more detail.

Your leveraged income exceeds your monthly expenses

This is what I define as the first level of financial independence. Your first major financial goal is to get to the point where you don't have to trade your time for the income that covers your mortgage or rent, bills and general expenditure. Successful businesses have to make a profit, but sustainability is what gives you a long-term future. It's the difference between only being as good as your last deal and having a product or service that is in constant demand.

For example, property development can make you good money, but then you've got to do it all over again. If you've got a profitable buy-to-let strategy, it can keep going and provide a sustainable income stream which is not dependent on you for its daily running. It's a system which may ultimately be overseen by you, but it generates profit whether you're there or not.

An HMO portfolio can allow you to achieve that first level of financial independence relatively quickly. But to establish the kind of property business that is effective in delivering leveraged income consistently, you need to ensure your business model is robust. And before you can do that, you need to make sure your financial blueprint – the way you are programmed to think about and manage money – is aligned with success and wealth.

At this point, if you haven't already read Robert Kiyosaki's *Rich Dad, Poor Dad*, make sure it's the next book you read. It's one of the most widely-read books in its field and is often referred to as the most successful financial book of all time. It addresses the proven fact that unless you make sure you think and behave like a rich person, you will never achieve long-term wealth.

One of the observations Kiyosaki makes is that most people earn an income from working and then use this money to live by paying for their expenses. This leads to the proverbial 'rat race' syndrome where people are forced to go out to work just to maintain their current standard of living. Kiyosaki asserts that wealthy people buy assets which generate income and their living expenses are covered by the proceeds of these assets. The enormous benefit to you of mastering and executing this approach is that it enables you to step off life's rat race treadmill for good, because you no longer have to trade your time for money.

Multiple streams of income

One of the great things about HMOs is that they have multiple units, so if one tenant leaves, you still have the income from the other units, compared with when a tenant leaves a single-occupancy property. Having said that, your property business is at its most robust when you have a balanced portfolio. Every great entrepreneur understands the sense in having multiple streams of income (MSIs), which can be different businesses and/or strands in the same business. The principle is that should one or two streams suffer at any point, the others will carry any shortfall and enable you to keep all your business interests running.

Imagine a diving board that's supported by one pillar at one end. When you put any force on the other end, it's going to bend right down, collapsing if the downward force is too great. I use that as a metaphor for creating wealth: if you've only got one business and one source of income, and something bad happens to that, you're in big trouble. If the diving board is supported by multiple pillars, it can withstand far more downward pressure. The same principle applies to your financial security.

In property, having MSIs generally means making investments which will bring different rewards at different times. I would guide most people to look primarily for an income-producing portfolio so they can give up the 'day job', and HMOs provide exactly that.

If you have experience and are confident that you can, with support, branch out into other property investment strategies, then you may also want to look for options which will give periodical lump-sum cash injections into your property business. These can come from a variety of different sources, such as:

- Refurbishing a property and selling it on for a profit

- Developing a property and selling it for a profit

- Achieving planning gain – adding value to a plot/ plots by securing development rights

- Adding value to commercial property by negotiating longer and more profitable leases, possibly through refurbishment

- Sourcing properties and development opportunities for a finder's fee

- Self-building – building a single-personal residence, subsequently selling or remortgaging to release some, or all, of the equity

There are so many ways you can make money from property – both residential and commercial – each of which require specialist knowledge to get the best returns, both now and in the future. But as long as you take the right advice, you should find yourself with a varied, exciting and profitable property business.

Your exit strategy

Too many people embark on new business ventures without really focusing on the end game – where they want to be, when, and how they're going to achieve the desired result in that timeframe. In property, people fail to consider their exit strategy.

Exit strategies will depend on your investment strategy, which is influenced by why you want to invest in property in the first place. Start with a long-term personal financial planning strategy, and then your business and property strategy should fit into that.

Your exit options will depend on a number of factors: your broader financial goals with regards to pension provision, legacy and inheritance planning. Are you planning on leaving property to your children, living off the income during retirement or paying down debt and selling up to give yourself a cash lump sum? Remember that over any long-term period, anything can happen, and circumstances can change, so have a good financial advisor on speed dial.

You need to do a lot of due diligence when you're investing in property, and it's important not to be blinkered in your strategies – yes, have them, but be prepared to adapt, because the property market is not a rigid thing. Sensible investing is making sure you have options and exit strategies. Although, if you've got a highly cash-flow-positive property, you're unlikely to ever want to sell it, the ideal position is that there's more than one way to make money from the investment. Make sure it stacks up well for income, but also look at what you could achieve in terms of lump-sum or multiple benefits.

For example, one of my buy-to-let houses is a very profitable eight-bedroom HMO that has a good plot with the potential to be split to build a new bungalow. Applying for planning permission will use a small proportion of the existing property's cash flow, but if planning is granted, it means I can sell the investment on for a large lump-sum profit or develop the plot. If it's not, I still have an investment that will continue to give me an excellent monthly income.

Protect your downside

There are many reasons why property is a great investment, not least of which is you can structure your business in a highly tax-efficient way. A big mistake that many investors make is not engaging a competent accountant, and if you don't have the right professional advice, you may find that over 40% of your hard-earned money goes to the Chancellor of the Exchequer.

There are many ways of legally reducing the tax that you pay on profits you make, both simple and sophisticated, so make sure you choose an accountant who understands the specific business you are in and has the right qualifications. Ask for references from their other clients who are in the same business as/a similar business to you, and bear in mind that this is certainly a situation where paying for the right advice is worth every penny. Platinum work with some of the best tax advisors in the UK and overseas, who keep us and our franchise partners one step ahead of this constantly changing market.

Summary

In this chapter, we've covered:

- Making sure you know what you're aiming for and choosing a strategy that will help you achieve your lifestyle goals

- Ensuring your business strategy fulfils the principles of the Holy Grail and Strategy checklist

- Working towards building a business that doesn't require you to trade your time for money

- Aiming to build MSIs

- Engaging a competent accountant

- Having realistic and achievable exit strategies

A great investment will have multiple angles for making a profit. These are the ones to look for and buy, but make sure you analyse the potential downsides before making your move. There can be several, which I'll explain in detail in the next chapter.

CHAPTER 5

MISTAKE #2 –
NOT PROTECTING
YOUR DOWNSIDE

Risk is my favourite word. While that might sound unusual coming from a property investor and entrepreneur, risk meant I learned the hard way about what can happen when you don't protect your downside.

The worst fear that many people have is starting a business that fails, meaning they lose their home, have to put a business into liquidation, and the ultimate sacrifice is bankruptcy. I was one step away from bankruptcy, and what saved me was my family home. Ever since that time, I have been hypersensitive to risk. In fact, on a daily basis, I am constantly asking myself what can go wrong.

So, what can go wrong when it comes to property investment specifically? There are a number of factors that are worth looking at in more detail.

The biggest risk is you

I'll come on to what I generally perceive as the most common external risks in a moment (and how you have some power to control their impact), but first I want to highlight what I consider to be the biggest overall risk, and that is you. From an internal point of view – the things within your control – it's down to you what strategy you follow, which property you buy and where, the builder you employ, the tenants you find and how effectively you manage the property, etc. But it's not just decisions you make about your property business that can have the greatest impact on its success.

Just think for a moment what could happen in your life that you can't necessarily control. Too many times, I have witnessed unfortunate events like divorce, illness and death resulting not only in emotional hardship for families, but also an added pressure when it comes to the management of a property business.

Death and taxes are the two certainties in life, and failure to plan for the worst from a personal perspective means that should something awful happen, you have no contingency plan in place. I call it the bus test. As morbid as it sounds, what would happen if you got run over by a bus and were hospitalised or, worse, died? Do your significant others know enough about your affairs? Do you have an up-to-date will? Have you documented an exit strategy? Do you have proper life and critical illness cover in place to prevent your family from experiencing financial hardship as well as grief if you are no longer around?

Few people talk about these kinds of risk, but they are real and need to be mitigated.

External risks

Aside from factors within your control, there are external risks to your property business. The most common model for analysing macro-risks in business is the PESTLE model – political, economic, social, technological, legal, environmental.

I'm not going to go into a huge amount of detail, but it's definitely worth thinking about what's happening, or what could happen, in the wider world, and then looking at it from your own personal circumstances. For example, is there likely to be a change in government that could cause uncertainty in the market or result in legislative change? How available are buy-to-let mortgages and what is the current tax landscape?

Is renting becoming more socially acceptable or are more people moving towards homeownership? Will there be any new environmental policies that require you to make your properties more energy efficient, and at what cost?

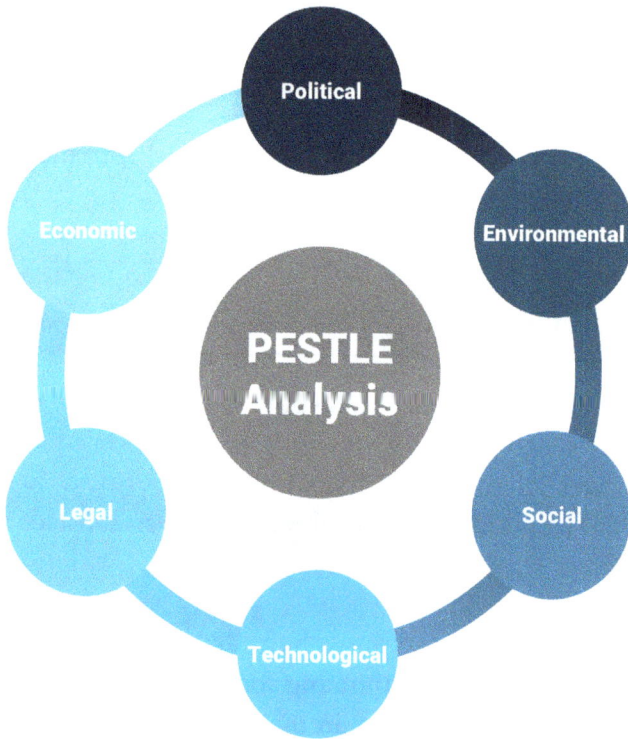

Fig 5.1: The PESTLE Analysis

Some things you just can't foresee. In 2001 when I nearly lost everything, I had no idea there was going to be an outbreak of Foot-and-mouth disease that prevented my business partner and me from going on land and building ropes courses. It killed our business. It's hard to predict external events, so having a robust business model that protects against the likely downsides is of fundamental importance.

Take advice and speak to other people who have done what you want to do. Ask how they mitigated these risks. Remember, standing on the shoulders of giants – utilising mentors – is the best way to maximise your chances of success.

Let's now look at three major external factors that people consider to be the biggest risks when investing in property:

- A property market crash resulting in negative equity

- Interest-rate rises pushing up monthly mortgage payments

- Void periods, where the units are untenanted and there's little or no rent coming in

As an HMO buy-to-let investor, you can generate cash flow. Cash flow is what can protect you against these threats, which is why I don't recommend starting your property investment journey with any of the other strategies I detailed earlier, because they won't produce a PSI.

Cash flow is king

Many years ago, I found out the hard way that if you don't have cash flow, you don't have a business. And that's a lesson that's since been learned the hard way by far too many other people. A lot of investors focused their entire business model, prior to the financial crisis, on capital appreciation. While the long-term viability and profitability in property investing as a business is unquestionable, once their short-term capital gain was taken away, many buy-to-let investors and developers were ruined. A lack of available finance compounded the issue.

When there is a correction in the property market and capital values decline, the people most at risk are those with a high level of gearing. If we look at the past two corrections, on average UK property values declined by about 15%. If you had a 95% loan-to-value (LTV) mortgage and property values went down by 15%, then you would have 10% negative equity and that's not a good place to be.

For example, one couple I spoke to in mid-2008 had a portfolio of twenty new-build apartments and small houses which were originally running at an average of £100 a month gross profit. The properties had all been expected to rise quickly in value, but in fact had become a massive millstone around their necks and they were cash-negative to the tune of £3,000 a month, with serious negative equity. The ways out of a situation like that are not attractive:

- Keep subsidising the portfolio, if possible, in the vain hope that it will recover

- Try to sell the properties, but accept that the sale price will probably be below the amount you owe on the mortgage so you'll need to pay a top-up to the lender

- Default on the mortgage and allow the properties to be repossessed, which will result in a financial loss and a bad credit rating, and the likelihood that getting another mortgage or any kind of credit will be impossible for many years

The first two options depend on an investor having a serious amount of capital or income that they're prepared to lose, while the third is, unfortunately, the only option available to most people. So how can you be as sure as possible that you will never find yourself in that position?

One way to mitigate this risk is not to gear too highly. I typically recommend a maximum of 75% LTV, possibly 80% in certain circumstances. Then, despite a property market crash being outside of your control, you have an income-producing strategy. If capital values do fall, you are able to trade through, keep the property and continue to make positive cash flow until the market bounces back. In this model, I assume zero capital growth forever. What would the numbers look like if you disregarded capital uplift? How would your portfolio perform?

Also think about your exit strategy. If you did need to sell for any particular reason, would you be able to? Who would you sell to and what price could you get?

Negative cash flow can be caused by not investing in a high-cash-flow strategy in the first place, but also by an interest rate rise. At best, it will put a dent in your profit, unless you are able to raise additional capital to achieve a lower LTV. You need to stress test your portfolio and work out what would happen if the borrowing rates were 5%, 6% or higher. If you know you can withstand, say, 10% interest rates before you are into negative cash flow, then you have a nice buffer. That's what Platinum Property Partners aim for.

If you're unable to remortgage because there's no capital appreciation, LTV rates have dropped or the fees outweigh the savings, having monthly cash flow is the only thing that can keep your business profitable.

Finally, if your tenant leaves and you have a month or two with nothing coming into the business, that's a serious problem, because you've still somehow got to fund the mortgage and any monthly bills. While void periods are on the decline as demand for rental properties continues to outweigh supply, the National Landlords Association still recommends planning for two months a year to cover voids and bad debts. That's a far cry from the 97% occupancy I recommend you aim for, but it's good downside planning.

When I moved into investing in residential property seriously, I was determined to make sure that the potential downsides in my new property business were covered, long term. Capital appreciation is not a 'strategy'. It's nice to be able to remortgage as and when possible and know that your long-term future is secure, but if property is going to be your primary business, it has to be profitable *today*, ie generating a consistent, reliable and secure monthly profit.

Your biggest asset

If you ask people what their biggest asset is, most will reply, 'My home', but nine times out of ten they're wrong. What they're not thinking about – and I'll freely admit it's something that I didn't really consider myself until I started investing professionally – is that property is only a true asset if it's servicing its own debt. If you have a sizeable mortgage and use part of your salary to pay it every month, the slightly uncomfortable reality is that your home is probably your biggest liability.

But that's just a fact of life, isn't it – we work to service our cost of living? That's certainly the traditional way of looking at life, and the majority of people do go to work every day to pay the monthly bills. But the whole underlying principle of your business life is to create leveraged income – establish streams of revenue which cover your monthly outgoings and continue regardless of whether you are there or not, ie you're not trading your time for money. Property can be the main income stream for you.

I make sure that every buy-to-let property I or my partners buy is truly an asset. It must not only service its own debt, but also bring in a high enough level of profit that we can draw an income and are well insulated against market fluctuations and interest-rate rises. Achieving such significant cash flow from properties is fairly straightforward, but it's certainly not easy. The people who thought their fortune was there on a plate and they could get very rich for relatively little effort are the people who are floundering now. Be under no illusion that what I'm going to talk about next is not a 'get rich quick' strategy – it's a 'get rich safely' approach and it requires effort, particularly for the first couple of years. Or, if you prefer, you can outsource the work to others who know what they are doing.

Achieving high cash flow to protect your downside

By far the best and most reliable way to maximise your rental income and profit from a property is to invest in HMOs. A typical HMO might be a four-bedroom three-reception-room family home which has been divided up into six individually let bedrooms, one communal reception room, a kitchen and two bathrooms – or, if the property allows, several en-suite bedrooms (aim for a minimum of one bathroom for every four people).

If you want to attract the best tenants who will pay the highest rent, you need to put in some effort and make sure you're offering high-quality housing. There is huge demand in most parts of the country from young working adults looking for somewhere equivalent in standard to a family home or a decent hotel, and that demand is growing. If you've seen the TV programme *Friends*, it's that kind of set-up: twenty-somethings, all with their own bedrooms, sharing the other facilities. Today's discerning house sharers also expect a cleaner and high-speed broadband to be provided. If you can meet a certain standard and treat the people living in your house in a decent way, you should find they will behave decently in return.

Unfortunately, there's still a way to go before the general population loosens up on its preconception that

HMOs equal louts and layabouts who cause endless trouble for landlords and the neighbourhood. One of my franchise partners who is investing in HMOs in Gloucestershire is a respectable man and operating entirely by the book, but shortly after he'd completed on an early purchase, the neighbours complained to the council about his plans. They even got a story published in the local paper, shrieking that he was going to lower the tone of the neighbourhood and create a dangerous environment by turning houses into drug dens.

That was an extreme case, but you may come across and need to overcome a great deal of suspicion and objection. This 'drugs baron' (as I jokingly call him now) has since received apologies from most of the neighbours who complained, some of whom have openly admitted that the kind of young working people he has renting rooms are probably less trouble than a 'normal' family with teenage children might have been.

There have also been cases where local authorities are clueless. In one case where a franchise partner was turning an old nursing home into a twelve-bedroom HMO near Liverpool, he had to work with the HMO officer to educate them on standards and policies because they had no idea. There were only six HMOs in the area that they knew of, and up until then, they'd never been proactively approached by a landlord.

The majority of people I speak to are quick to say that they don't want to get involved with lots of tenants because of the amount of hassle they create, like phone calls at all hours about blocked toilets. There will be some problems, but the huge upside is you're benefiting from two to four times the level of rental income you would have got from letting the property as a single unit. Done in the right way, an HMO is a system you can hand over to someone else who you employ to manage your portfolio. But I recommend you learn the ropes yourself first.

Good for landlords, good for tenants

By acknowledging there's work to be done when you look at the figures, you put everything into perspective. Operating multi-tenanted professional-let properties, which we'll look at more closely in due course, should mean a profit of around £20,000 per annum, per property for you – even after you've paid all costs including mortgage, bills and maintenance, and accounting for voids. You can't expect to do nothing for £1,600+ a month profit, but if you set up and run your business in the right way, as your portfolio grows, you will be able to afford to take on first a part-time, and then a full-time property manager to handle all this for you, at which point all that should be required of you is a few hours a week. Your cash-positive HMO portfolio becomes your almost passive leveraged PSI.

The reason for making such an effort with HMOs comes down to protecting your downside. You tend to break even or run a small profit by letting a property as a single unit or handing the entire letting and management of it over to an agency. The smaller your profit margins, the more exposed and vulnerable you are when shifts in the property and mortgage markets occur.

By letting five or more individual rooms in a property, you will easily double, if not quadruple, the income you would have got from letting it to one tenant, and the added bonus is the likelihood of having a whole property vacant at any time is virtually nil. Rooms one to four tend to cover your mortgage and bills, and then rooms five onwards are more or less your profit. Professionals in this sector of the market, like my franchise partners, operate at a minimum of 97% occupancy most of the time. If one room out of six is empty, it only has one-sixth of an impact on occupancy, compared with a single let which is 100% empty.

There is nothing about the HMO model that will make a bigger difference to profit potential than number of bedrooms. For a bedroom in the South-East, rent is between £550 and £900 per month. With an average price of £700 per bedroom, annual rental income from one extra bedroom is more than £8,000 per year. Take a look at the graphic below to see how just four numbers over a ten-year period can make a huge difference. (The graphic shows the compound impact of these numbers based on five six-bedroom properties over a period of ten years.)

1	2	3	4	What happens when these four elements combine...
£15 per room per week £234,000	97% vs 90% occupancy £127,400	1 extra room per property £301,600	1 extra property £200,000	£863,000

Of course, it's not just landlords who will benefit financially from investing in HMOs. Demand for high-quality and affordable accommodation is on the up, and HMOs enable tenants to save money when compared with renting on their own – £1,600 more per year when I last conducted some market research.

Factors to consider

For too long, people have been fed the idea that they can get rich and stay rich through property investing with no money, skill or effort, and it's simply not true. It's not an easy route to go down; HMOs require hard work and a solid strategy behind them, and it's not a market for amateurs. But if you're prepared for that, you'll end up with a virtually recession-proof income.

I can't stress enough the importance of spending time talking to people who make their living from this kind of investing, because it can be a minefield. There are a huge number of legislative issues governing what can and can't be done (which I will come on to later), and if you're not even aware of what questions you should be asking, who you should be asking, and what answers you're looking for, you can get in a serious mess. But assuming you're working with the right people, are prepared to put in some hard work at the start and are adequately funded, there are potentially great rewards.

CASE STUDY

Here is an example of a highly cash-positive HMO bought by a PPP franchise partner in the South in 2016.

Property purchase price	£320,000
Amount borrowed	£244,800
(75% plus arrangement fee)	
Investor's capital input	
Deposit (25%)	£80,000
Refurbishment and purchase costs	£65,800
Total capital input	£145,800
Single property income – monthly	
Income (rent for six rooms at £600 per month plus fees and minus voids)	£3,572
Expenditure – monthly	

Mortgage interest	£979
Interest cost of investor's capital (assumes 2% on £145,800)	£243
Maintenance	£108
Property-related operating costs	£500
Platinum franchise support (5% +VAT)	£214
Total expenses	£2,044
Monthly gross profit	£1,528
Annual gross profit	£18,336

The gross profit figure has been calculated as a minimum and can be elevated with things like laundry income and by having double occupancy in one or two of the rooms, subject to obtaining any necessary permissions from the local council.

Of course, an important differentiator is location. In London and the South-East, the purchase price is going to be high, but so is the rental income. If the HMO is in the Midlands, the North or some of the more affordable areas of the country, then the purchase price and rents will be lower respectively.

Platinum have recently had some franchise partners join us in Teesside. They were worried that with them not being in a big city or near a major hub of employment, the fact that housing stock was relatively cheap compared with southern regions and people could afford to rent on their own, HMOs wouldn't work. They soon realised that if you do it right, you can make HMOs work anywhere within an hour of where you live.

There are other variables which are outside your control, chiefly interest rates and maximum LTV levels, but the beauty of this model is that if interest rates fall, your cash flow increases, and if they rise, you are well insulated because of the high level of profit you're making.

If you believe interest rates might rise, you can opt for a fixed-rate mortgage, so that you can keep better control of your monthly outgoings. With a lower LTV, your capital input is going to be higher, but your cash flow will be better. As time passes and if you want to, you'll be able to remortgage. As I did with a number of my properties over time, you may be able to release all your capital in the long term and still reap a good monthly profit, giving you an infinite return on your investment.

Summary

In this chapter, we've covered:

- One of the biggest risks to your business is you making the wrong or no decision

- Being aware of and analysing potential external risks

- Concentrating on achieving high monthly income – cash flow is king

- Thinking about your biggest asset and how you use it to create leveraged income

- Being prepared to put in hard work (or outsource it)

- Understanding that HMOs are the best and most reliable property investments to maximise rental income

If the financial metrics I've covered in this chapter have confused you, then you are not alone. We'll go into the numbers in more detail in the next chapter, because having a highly cash-flow-positive property investment is one thing, but it will never be sustainable if you don't understand the numbers.

CHAPTER 6

MISTAKE #3 –
NOT UNDERSTANDING
THE NUMBERS

'Failing to plan is planning to fail.'
— Benjamin Franklin

It never ceases to amaze me how many people don't understand what's involved in property investment or why they're doing it. It's common knowledge that the majority of investors own just one or two buy-to-let properties and are landlords through pure circumstance. Many simply had a property they could rent out or inherited one.

In a bid to add some credence to my own thoughts, I conducted an independent survey through Platinum of UK buy-to-let investors and found that only three in ten (28%) deliberately set out to purchase a buy-to-let property, and an astonishing 93% had no five-year plan for their investment. Fewer than half of investors (43%) said they fully understood what they were doing when they entered buy-to-let; fewer than one in five did a lot of research (18%); one in ten trusted luck; and a quarter of investors sought no advice and carried out no research on which property to buy.

What was even more shocking was the overwhelming confusion about the key financial metrics of property investment. While 23% of UK landlords don't measure the return on their buy-to-let investments at all, those who do aren't measuring their portfolio performance effectively. Nearly a fifth (17%) had no idea of the value of their gross annual yield, and 14% revealed that they don't understand the term because they said they had a negative gross yield, which is a mathematical impossibility.

The results of this survey, and many others, proved to me that there is a striking and worrying level of financial illiteracy among the general population and property-investment community, which is probably because many people don't understand their numbers from a personal perspective, let alone a business perspective.

A while ago, I completed a financial planning training workshop attended by twenty independent financial advisors (IFAs), all of whom were taking a financial planning certificate. The lecturer asked everyone in the room who asked their clients about their annual income and expenditure, both personally and for their family, and their assets and liabilities, ie their net worth. And not a single hand went up apart from mine. It stunned me into silence. How can you dispense financial advice if you don't know the most basic financial information?

If you want to create a plan for the future, you have to know where you're starting from. This is why goal setting is so important in the first instance, both personally and professionally, but it must be backed up by a financial plan. When I start mentoring and partnering with people in property or other businesses, I always insist that they complete a simple one-page spreadsheet that shows their income, expenditure, assets and liabilities. It gives them a snapshot of where they are now, and then they can plan where they want to get to and how to get there.

Your personal net worth

If you don't know your personal income and expenditure and net worth, then you really need to address that, because property and business is a game played by the numbers. It doesn't mean you need to have a degree in mathematics or be a chartered accountant, but for sure you need to have a level of financial competence that allows you to understand the past, the present and the future. In effect, you need to become the CEO of You Ltd. If you don't understand how to manage your own finances and plan your financial future, you'll struggle with running your own business and it will greatly increase the level of risk you expose yourself to.

I'd urge you to create a spreadsheet which contains the following details:

- Your **monthly income** – including any property income

- Your **monthly expenditure** – broken down into loan/credit-card obligations and other living expenses

- Your monthly income minus your monthly expenditure gives you your **monthly and annual cash flow** figures

- Your **assets** – property, business assets, vehicles, investments and savings

- Your **liabilities** – outstanding mortgage balances, total credit-card debt and loans

- Your assets minus your liabilities gives you your **personal net worth**

Rather than you having to reinvent the wheel, I'd be happy to give you a net worth calculator I created over a decade ago.

Visit https://platinumpropertypartners.co.uk/free-resources to download your free copy. You can also use the online net worth calculator I created here – www.networthcalculator.co.uk

Needless to say, your personal net worth should be a positive, not a negative figure.

In his book *The Millionaire Next Door*, Thomas Stanley suggests your net worth should be roughly equivalent to:

$$\text{Target net worth} = \frac{\text{Age} \times \text{your pre-tax salary}}{10}$$

While it's certainly not an exact science, it's not a bad benchmark. Although your properties might not contribute significantly to your net worth if they're highly leveraged, you want to aim to put a decent proportion of your income into assets, rather than simply spending it on 'disposables'.

I handed my spreadsheet to my private banking manager when I was looking to move some accounts, and he said that in twenty-five years he had never had a customer give him such a simple, clear and accurate statement of their personal financial situation. If you know how to do the same for your business and your personal life, you'll be one step ahead when you come to deal with lenders and/or passive investors. And remember that your personal and business finances will have some crossover, so the more detail you understand about both, the more effectively you'll be able to run them.

Effective measurement of buy-to-let portfolio performance

'If you can't measure it, you can't manage it.'
— Robert Kaplan

When it comes to knowing the numbers involved in investing in residential property, you need to take into account several factors when considering the profitability of an individual deal. Up front, you need to consider your purchasing costs and capital input (briefly detailed in the last chapter). These will include:

- Deposit

- Purchase fees (Stamp Duty, legal fees, valuation, mortgage and broker etc)

- Refurbishment/improvement costs

- Planning, licensing and building regulation costs

- Furnishings

Then you'll need to understand what rental income you can achieve minus monthly expenditure to get your monthly gross profit, including:

- Mortgage interest payments

- Other loan interest

- Utilities

- Council tax

- Maintenance

- Voids

The most common metric in residential property is gross yield. In basic terms, this is the annual rental income divided by the value of the property. A better and more accurate way to calculate gross yield is to work out the rental income as a proportion of purchase costs plus any refurbishment costs.

While this is interesting as an intellectual exercise, it doesn't factor in the return on your money. There's a big difference between buying a property for cash versus using a mortgage and that needs to be taken into account. Focus most on return on capital. How much money have you got tied up in property or business, and what return are you getting on that capital?

Return on equity (ROE) is a fundamental of investing and one which you must understand. If you invest

£200,000 into an HMO which brings you £20k profit a year, that's a 10% return on equity (ROE) – the profit divided by the capital invested. If you are then able to refinance the property because you have added value through improvements, or it has gone up with capital appreciation, and pull out £100,000 of your £200,000, only £100,000 will be left invested. And then even if your cash flow drops slightly to, say, £18,000 a year because of higher interest costs on a bigger mortgage, you will be making an 18% ROE (£18k/£100k). You will have nearly doubled how hard your invested cash is working for you and your profit on a pound-for-pound basis.

Make sense? Don't worry if not. This takes time for some people to understand if they are not from a property background, so just know it is a vital concept to grasp. In my opinion it is the single most valuable key performance indicator (KPI) there is for HMO investing.

KPIs

In any business, you need KPIs that you want to measure, so implement a system for doing this consistently. But despite property being a business, many landlords fail to see it that way.

KPIs are the metrics by which you analyse opportunities and deals and measure success. Just like having goals, every individual should know what their KPIs are for both their business and their personal life. There are certain KPIs that are common to most businesses and others which will be particular to you, and you set your own KPIs according to what you're trying to achieve.

Any sound business will produce monthly management accounts. These will include:

- Profit and loss (P&L)

- Balance sheet

- Cash flow and/or P&L forecast

- Budgets versus actuals report

The first two reports are historical while the second two also look into the future, based on your assumptions and what you expect to happen. Without these tools in place, you are essentially running your business with a blindfold on. Like it or not, business is a game played primarily by the numbers. If you don't understand your numbers, you don't really have a proper business. While you can delegate some of the financial work, you have to understand your figures and have the right kind of people supporting you. Too many people rely on bookkeepers and accountants without appreciating that they can only be as good as the instructions they receive from the business owner, so don't expect an accountant to make the right decisions for you.

I learned this lesson the hard way in 1997 when I employed a full-time bookkeeper in my construction business. Rather than ensuring that she understood the key aspects of how the business operated and its particular complexities of tax, national insurance and other matters, I just let her get on with things, so she did little more than file annual accounts and answer the odd query as it came up. Neither she nor I were proactive, and because I didn't know what questions to ask, I never got the answers I needed.

After eighteen months, the business was hit with an unexpected and large corporation tax bill. Shortly after this, I also had to pay £19,000 of tax and national insurance for sub-contractors who had not paid these themselves. From that point on, I made sure to learn all about the financial management of businesses. It took time and effort, but it has rewarded me many times over. I would advise you to do the same if you want to be successful.

In addition to financial KPIs, you can measure almost anything you like. At Platinum, we have invested thousands of hours and hundreds of thousands of pounds over the years in developing measurement and management systems that act as dashboards for our partners.

In their simplest form, all businesses have three main functions:

- Sales and marketing: the activities involved in selling and promoting an organisation's goods and/or services
- Operations: ongoing recurring activities involved in the running of a business for the purpose of producing value for the stakeholders
- Finance/HR/admin: matters related to money within the business

Here is a small selection of non-financial KPIs that my team and partners measure weekly in their property businesses:

- Number of new tenant enquiries
- Number of tenant viewings
- Number of rented rooms
- Amount of late rental payments
- Amount of late rental payments against deposits held
- Number of rooms becoming vacant in the next month

There are numerous benefits in correctly tracking KPIs like those I've listed. For example, I know that on average, six incoming enquiries will usually lead to three viewings, which in turn will lead to one rented room. Therefore, if my property business has two empty rooms coming up in the next month, my team knows to generate at least twelve enquiries to ensure they are filled quickly.

KPIs are some of the leading indicators for your rental portfolio and they assist you in ensuring that your occupancy levels stay as high as possible. If you only rely on historical financial management accounts, it's equivalent to driving by looking in the rear-view mirror. To be effective, you need to have a range of KPIs that suit your particular business and situation. I strongly advise you to determine what business KPIs you want to measure and then implement a system for doing this consistently.

An example of a less common KPI my business partners and I measure relates to the amount of time we have to invest in the business on a weekly and monthly basis as a percentage of our overall time. Our goal is for this KPI percentage figure to be constantly reducing over time, while our profitability and income KPI figures are rising, so we know we're on track for growing the business while making it more of a leveraged income stream. Strive to get maximum results for a reducing amount of time commitment, which means knowing as early as possible in the life of your business what you need to measure and making sure you have a system in place that will accurately record those KPIs.

If you just have financial KPIs and they're not related to time, quality of life and health, then you can end up getting great financial profit, cash flow and equity growth, but that's no good if you've got to work seven days a week, fifty-two weeks a year, and your health is declining in the process. Take a holistic approach to your business and understand what your personal KPIs are, because a great motivation for creating and growing a property business is to have a better quality of life and standard of living, so you're able to give back and help others more.

As an aside, the French government proposed that countries should not just measure gross domestic product (GDP) and other financial aspects of the economy, but also include the health and happiness of their populations as a better measure of the success of the country's performance. If you forget to measure how your division of time and energy is progressing, you can easily lose focus and end up on a path which is out of synch with your ultimate goal, and then you won't understand exactly why, where and how it went wrong.

Administration systems and procedures

Before you jump into buying properties, you need to understand where your administration strengths and capabilities lie, and what to do about your weaknesses. There is a lot of administration involved, from setting up suitable paper-filing systems, to recording expenditure and tracking invoices and receipts related to property refurbishment and management, to reconciling bank statements and being able to produce accurate P&L statements and balance sheets. If you've never done anything like this, you need to speak to people who have, and make a decision about whether you learn how to do it for yourself or outsource a lot of the work.

To operate your business in-house, you need to have basic bookkeeping skills and be able to work in an organised and systemised way, and it helps a great deal if you are computer literate. If you're naturally quick on the uptake with computer systems and good with figures, it's probably cost-effective for you to handle everything yourself, and just outsource your end-of-year accounts to an accountant, but if getting up to speed is going to take a large investment of your time and money, I would suggest you employ a bookkeeper early on.

You might already have an accountant, a bookkeeper and a tax advisor, but check whether they've dealt with clients who have property investments and make sure they have some experience in the field. There are certain requirements and issues that are particular to property investment, and if a bookkeeper, for example, has never dealt with a property business, they may well not be aware they should be recording things in a certain way. Similarly, your tax advisor might be excellent at dealing with personal and corporate tax, but if they haven't dealt with a lot of property investment-related businesses, they may not be up to date with the most tax-efficient ways to structure your affairs.

Unfortunately, many people find it hard to obtain good advice on property investment. It just isn't available at present in the way that professionals such as IFAs and stockbrokers advise on other forms of investment. Advice on standard buy-to-let investment is, of course, achievable through reading books on property investment and undertaking extensive research, but there's no better way to learn than from people with hands-on experience. It might be another cost that you have to factor into your number crunching, but I can almost guarantee (and I rarely make guarantees) that the right advice will be money well spent.

'The best investment you can make, is an investment in yourself.'
— Warren Buffett

Don't leave things to chance

Buy-to-let property is likely to be the biggest single investment for most investors, other than their family home, so it is essential you actively plan for and manage it. I'm sure there are few other investments you'd be comfortable making without at least an idea of how it's going to work for you, so the fact so many property investors are leaving their investments to chance is remarkable.

If you've become a buy-to-let investor almost accidentally through inheritance or changes of circumstance, you're unlikely at first to have a full understanding of the market. You certainly won't have had a chance to put together a plan of action. But that doesn't mean you should continue in the market without nailing down the direction you want your high-value investment to take – particularly if you want to maximise the income you're able to generate from it.

Finding the right property for your investment will maximise both capital growth and income. You are at great risk of not achieving the best return from your investment if you have no plan, no strategy, and no understanding of financial measures. Such an unplanned approach to buy-to-let investment is a huge gamble. Knowing what sort of property to buy, where to buy it and how much income will be generated will help you estimate your long-term ROE and annual profit more accurately. A good plan will include much more than many buy-to-let investors consider at present.

Firstly, setting financial goals that are aligned with your personal goals can help you determine what you hope to achieve through investing in property. Secondly, factor in all costs – refurbishment and maintenance costs as well as tenant sourcing and portfolio management. Thirdly, assess income and costs regularly to enable you to calculate your ROE and gross annual profit. This will also show how fluctuations in rent you're charging, fees you're paying and mortgage interest rates can affect these figures and how your KPIs are stacking up.

Last, but not least, work out how many properties you will need to achieve your financial goals and how you will fund your growth. If you're not planning on leveraging equity and think cash is the safest way to protect your downside, then you may not be maximising your chances of success.

Summary

In this chapter, we've covered:

- The need to be financially literate to invest in property

- Knowing your personal income and expenditure, assets and liabilities to get your net worth

- Understanding key financial measures and doing your calculations *before* you invest

- Setting KPIs

If numbers aren't your strength, ensure you have someone who can crunch them for you, but aim to have a decent level of understanding. I've never met a self-made wealthy person who is not good with numbers. Take heed!

CHAPTER 7

MISTAKE #4 – NOT UTILISING THE POWER OF LEVERAGE

'In the broad definition of the world, the word leverage simply means "the ability to do more with less".'
— Robert Kiyosaki

The term leverage can be used in a number of contexts which are all, in one way or another, relevant to your success in property investment. You can leverage the power of technology and systems and other people's time and skills, but for now, I am talking specifically about financial leverage in terms of investment. This is defined as 'the degree to which an investor or business is utilising borrowed money'. UK banks tend to refer to it as 'gearing'.

Leveraging is a key reason why property is probably the world's greatest money-making machine. Ask a bank for a loan of £50,000 to invest in the stock market and you'll be laughed out of the building, but ask for £50,000 towards the purchase of a £100,000 property and the strong likelihood is you'll get it, subject to affordability and/or rental income. Property has always been, and will almost certainly continue to be considered one of the world's safest investment vehicles, and that's why institutions and individual passive investors are so willing to lend against it. And that willingness of third parties to lend is what helps make us money.

Here is an example to demonstrate the power of leverage/gearing in property. If you already understand the concept, just skip over it, as I don't want to teach you to suck eggs!

If you invest £100,000 in a property with no mortgage, when the market goes up by 10%, you make an ROI of £10,000. But if you use that same £100,000 in capital as a 25% deposit on a £400,000 buy-to-let property, you get a £400,000 asset for just £100,000 of your own money. And when the property market goes up by 10%, you make £40,000 – a 40% ROI – because you don't just profit from the growth on your own money, you also profit from the growth on your mortgage lender's money.

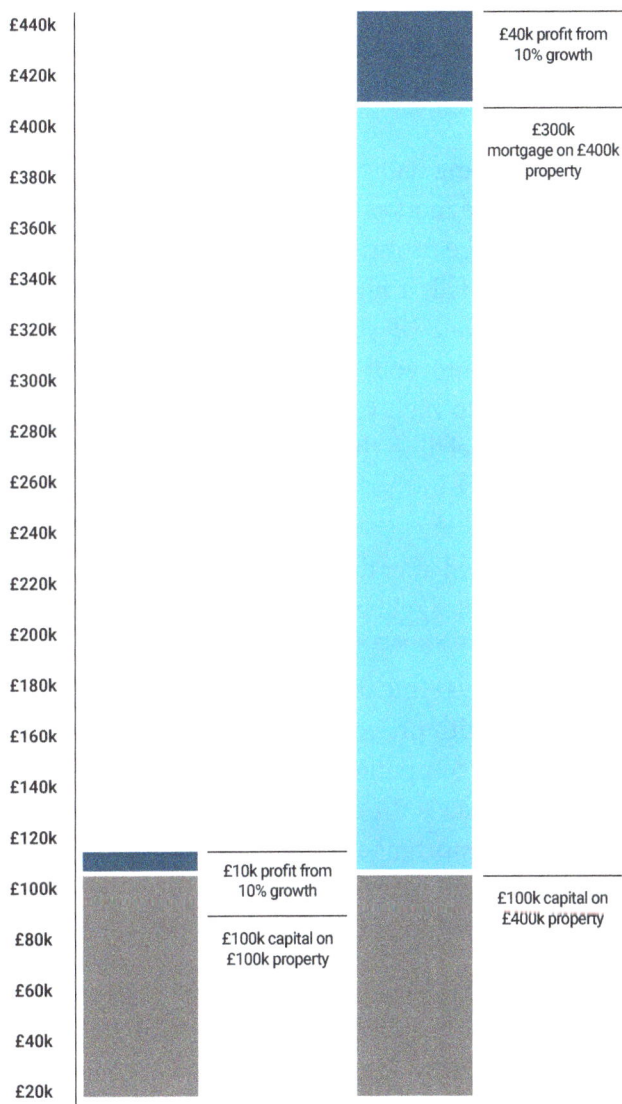

Fig 7.1: ROI and the power of leverage

(The financial examples in this chapter are simplified and ignore purchase/sale costs, tax, etc to make the broader points simpler.)

Leverage, or being highly geared, acts like a magnifying glass. When the market moves upwards – and in your favour – leverage massively improves your returns, but with a market fall, a high level of debt can leave you exposed, especially if you don't have adequate profit margins built into your investment model. If you are going to gear up highly then use a robust, proven and profitable model like the professional HMO strategy I detailed earlier in the book. Failure to do this caused thousands of highly geared investors to have their properties repossessed after the financial crisis, and is why so many are now struggling with the combination of:

- New tax laws – meaning private amateur landlords with property owned in their own names (Ltd companies excluded) can no longer deduct 100% of their finance costs (most commonly mortgage interest) as an expense before calculating taxable profit. The larger your mortgage payment, the more tax you will pay.

- Increased stress testing – many lenders are now stress testing the amount a buy-to-let investor wants to borrow against a 145% rental cover and 5% interest rate, so do your sums in advance and get advice from good brokers.

This has left many investors preferring to buy for cash, meaning their monthly profit will be higher, but ROE will be lower – and ROE is the number-one financial indicator to focus on. Buying for cash also means you'll have cash tied up in an illiquid asset, which prevents you from making further investments unless you are cash rich. Often, this decision comes down to not understanding the difference between good and bad debt.

Good vs bad debt

The first step to feeling comfortable with debt is understanding the difference between good and bad debt. In property, it comes down to ensuring you have assets, not liabilities. If by incurring debt you are creating an income stream – as is the case with highly cash-positive buy-to-let investing – that is good debt. The asset doesn't only cover the cost of servicing the debt (eg mortgage interest repayment) and any further associated costs (eg bills, tax etc), it provides a healthy profit on top, and if that's your situation, you've got yourself some good debt.

Bad debt is the reverse – it means you have to pay out yourself to service it. If you buy a new car on finance, for example, that's a bad debt. Not only does the product immediately depreciate, you also have to pay out interest every month.

In property terms, if you have to go to work to pay your mortgage, that is generally seen as bad debt. While capital appreciation will, over time, more than cover the interest you have to pay in the short term, if you were to lose your job and stop paying your mortgage today, you would be homeless. Most people's home, if they have a mortgage on it, is only giving them security of tenure (which is what many home-owners strive for) while they can afford to pay the mortgage, and therefore it is a liability.

If you're serious about being business-minded and using property as an investment tool to create financial independence for you and your family, then owning a property outright is simply holding you back and is a gross under-utilisation of your capital. As long as you are following a proven strategy, your quickest route to exponentially increasing your income is by leveraging borrowed finance.

In August 2007, when Amstrad's merger with BSkyB was announced, Lord Sugar told *The Sunday Times* he was planning to turn his attention to his property portfolio, which he deeply regretted not spending more time on in the 'golden' ten years from the mid-nineties.

Almost a decade on, it's reported he took home £181 million in dividends from property in one year, so it seems his attention paid off.[4] But if it's taken Lord Sugar all these years to appreciate the value of leverage, then you needn't feel too bad if the penny hasn't quite dropped for you until now either! I would emphasise that property needs to be leveraged *properly* because it's imperative that you do your homework and have a solid plan for servicing the debt you'll be taking on before you rush out and start looking to remortgage your home. This is where a good mortgage broker wouldn't go amiss. Again, it's a simple principle, but not an easy strategy to execute.

Financial independence

This is the key motivation for the vast majority of property investors, and it means different things to everyone. For some, simply reaching the first level of financial independence is enough, ie having your leveraged monthly income exceeding your monthly expenditure, so if your home mortgage payment, bills and all other outgoings add up to £2,000 a month, you need to be generating over £2,000 net income every month from a source which doesn't require you to trade your time for that money On a basic level, this could mean renting out some of your unused bedrooms/garage space. From an ROI point of view, you need to have the income-generating asset financially

---

4   www.telegraph.co.uk/business/2017/01/08/lord-sugar-enjoys-181m-dividend-property-empire/

leveraged as highly as possible, and you also need to be leveraging other people's time.

CASE STUDY: THE POWER OF LEVERAGE

Here's a real-life example of someone successfully using leverage in his property business. Back in 2013, Bill Mann was working in IT as a senior vice president for Visa Europe earning £100k+ a year. He'd always thought about starting his own business and investing in property, and in 2011, when Bill sadly lost his wife to cancer, he looked into investing some of his capital into single-occupancy buy-to-lets – literally handing them over to a letting agent to handle the rest. But being a numbers man, he realised it was hardly worth having all that capital tied up for little return.

Through his work, he'd met an existing franchise partner and decided to find out more about Platinum Property Partners. In 2013, he joined and, while working full time, had built a portfolio of three six-bedroom HMOs around the Upminster area of Essex within a year – the third taking only nine weeks from completion to fully tenanted. By this time, he'd replaced his salary.

Voluntary redundancy followed, and with no financial need to go back to work, Bill took the opportunity to focus on property full time. I say full time, but he told me that on a quiet week, when all he's doing is the bookkeeping, he'll spend just one hour on his property business; on a busier week, when there are maintenance issues to sort and tenant viewings or check-ins, he might work two full days.

A further three HMOs followed, Bill taking the approach of buying well-kept properties that needed little refurbishment and conversion work. On one property, he spent less than £20,000. He's also keen not to over leverage and, on average, mortgages the properties on a 65% LTV. His returns are between 15% and 27% across the portfolio; his monthly gross income is £11,000; and by the beginning of 2018, the value of his portfolio stood at just under £2 million.

It's not all been plain sailing for Bill, though. Firstly, he built half of his portfolio while working full time. He also manages every aspect of the business himself, but only because that's what he chooses to do. He could choose to outsource it, but at the time of writing, he is still enjoying it and it doesn't take much time. There will always be challenges with building and running a property business, no matter what strategy you follow and how much support you have (although that does make overcoming challenges a lot easier and cheaper). What he has achieved is the financial and time freedom to take control of his life and choose how he wants to spend his time.

Bill is now pursuing different property investment strategies and developing a diversified portfolio. More inspiring, though, is that fact that he has written two books that document how he overcame the trauma and tragedy of being in the same carriage as the 7/7 bomber in London in 2005 and losing his wife to rebuild his life and achieve fulfilment.

This all flies in the face of paid employment being a safe and solid option and debt a bad thing.

I work a lot because I love what I do. It's because I leverage other people's time and money to create my primary income streams that I can spend so much time away from 'the office'. If I was suddenly unable to work anymore, I know that I've already put the pieces in place to not have to worry about my family's financial security.

Sure, there are still times I get stressed out – I take on too much, or things outside my control go wrong and need to be dealt with, but on the whole, I am extremely blessed. And I take pleasure in helping others to have more choices, freedom and all-round success in their lives.

Leverage enables you to build a business which can essentially run without you, and it means your capital goes further. The more you earn, the more you can invest, and if you're leveraging correctly, your portfolio of assets will grow exponentially, as you use OPM and time to increase your own wealth.

Most of the richest people in the world built their wealth by firstly having huge amounts of debt, so if you have any negative thoughts about what it means to be wealthy, get over them! Forget megalomaniac workaholics; the new wave of wealthy people are 'philantropreneurs' – those who believe in sharing the wealth they create and making the world a better place. Paul Newman gave all the profits from his

'Newman's Own' range of foodstuffs to charity; Bill Gates has been funding medical advances in Third World countries for decades; and Facebook's Mark Zuckerberg and his wife Priscilla have pledged to give away 99% of their wealth to public interest causes. And remember, giving is not just about cash; you can give time, ideas, resources, etc.

Utilising leverage to create MSIs

Having MSIs is a fundamental concept in leveraging, but it does come with a health and wealth warning: don't start multiple businesses all at the same time! Early in my business building career, I perfectly understood the sense in having MSIs: if one business is going through a difficult time, for whatever reason, the other businesses would carry me through. I was (and still am) very ambitious and had great self-belief, so I started four different businesses within a twelve-month period, thinking if anyone could build an empire, it was me. All that happened was that I worked far too hard, became increasingly stressed and ended up exiting from three of the businesses.

New business ventures require you to dedicate a significant amount of your time, energy and money in the early days, and you can't possibly build anything meaningful if your attention is split in a lot of different directions. The best approach is to have a PSI

– the source of income that pays the bills and covers your basic needs – and then gradually build up other streams alongside it. If you correctly systemise your businesses and/or investments, you'll find them easier to manage, then you can leverage other people's time and effort, freeing up your time to concentrate on creating yet more streams of income and investments.

The beauty of property investing is that your MSIs can be all under the same umbrella, so a lot of your business support will probably be in place, making each 'start-up' easier. For example, if you have a few cash-positive buy-to-let properties up and running, you'll already know decent tradespeople and contractors – handyman, plumber, electrician, plasterer, painter etc – so if you decide to move into self-build, you've got a head start with a network of people to do the work for you. If you move into international investments, you'll already have a good understanding of the financial aspects of investing and the administrative systems in place for keeping track of management information.

The key is not losing sight of your PSI, and ensuring it continues to hold up as a solid foundation for your other income streams. If your PSI is at risk or you don't enjoy it, then you have a big challenge to solve. Finding and growing a new PSI quickly is of paramount importance to you in this situation, so you need to act fast.

Leveraging your property portfolio

To end this chapter, I want to talk a little about 'proper' leveraging. I'm assuming you are comfortable taking on some good debt to fund your property investment journey or portfolio growth, so you need to understand that there are different finance products for different types of strategies.

The lending structure for development or commercial investment, for example, is nothing like your residential mortgage on your home. And while standard buy-to-let and even HMO mortgages are similar, the fees and interest rates tend to be higher and there are more restrictions around age and the term of the mortgage, for instance.

It's also important to know that when you buy a property you intend to operate as an HMO, it's not likely to be one at the time of purchase. If you're looking to maximise the value of your investment by achieving development gains as well as a significant monthly income, you'll probably be buying a single-occupancy dwelling, or if you're more advanced and adventurous, maybe a small hotel or nursing home, so you won't be able to get an HMO mortgage because lenders won't lend you money on that basis if you don't have any income. This is where you need to speak to specialist mortgage brokers who can get a clear idea of your goals for the property, the capital and any other assets you have, to come up with a finance solution for you until you can remortgage on to a standard HMO product when the property is ready.

Summary

In this chapter, we've covered:

- Making sure you use leverage to acquire assets, not liabilities

- Embracing the idea of 'good debt'

- The first level of financial independence, which is when your leveraged income exceeds your expenditure

- Have a PSI, and then gradually building up MSIo alongside it

- Thinking of leverage as an accelerant for your timescale to achieving your financial and personal goals

CHAPTER 8

MISTAKE #5 –
CHOOSING THE WRONG
INVESTMENT LOCATION
AND PROPERTY

Another big mistake that property investors can make is choosing the wrong investment location and type of property by failing to do any competitor analysis and customer research upfront, whatever strategy they have chosen to follow.

Before I decided that I wanted to invest in professional HMOs (because I didn't yet know that they produced the highest income, lowest level of voids and good tenants), I was researching the 'where'. I spent two years reading various books, working one-to-one with mentors and flying all over the world, attending courses with the aim of seeing where I wanted to invest, and one of the locations that cropped up as a potential was Las Vegas. It just wasn't practical. I knew, having already set my personal and financial goals, that I didn't want to be passive. Nor did I want to expose myself, or my family's financial security, to currency and legal risks, or time and travel costs.

I then discovered the high-quality HMO model and needed to understand where it would work.

Where you decide to invest will be driven by a number of factors:

- Where will your strategy work in the world or country?

- What kind of lifestyle are you hoping to achieve and are you happy travelling all the time?

- Do you want to take on added currency, legal, travel and time risks?

There is no right or wrong. I made a lifestyle choice to find a strategy that could work within an hour of where I lived. I wanted to be close to my family and know the area in which I would be building my property business so that I could forge strong relationships with estate agents, surveyors, builders and tradespeople. So, like any sensible businessperson, I started by conducting a competitor analysis.

Analyse the competition

When I went to view twenty rooms in the local area, I was appalled by the poor quality of accommodation, and at the way I was treated and spoken to. On one particular occasion, I was asked to turn up outside a fish and chip shop at 6.30pm. When I got there, two other people were also waiting. A white van pulled up and a bloke wound down the window and asked if we were there to look at the room, telling us to jump in the back of the van. There were no seats or seatbelts, just paint pots, and he took us on an uncomfortable three-mile journey to a little suburb of Bournemouth.

When I walked through the door of the property, the stench hit me. There were two hairy builders on the sofa, drinking Special Brew and watching TV; the kitchen was a mess, the bedroom was even worse. Out of the four bedrooms, one was available. It was a double room with cigarette burns all over the carpet, a double bed with a stained mattress in one corner and a wardrobe in the other. There was only one shared bathroom, which was also disgusting.

The bloke told us the room was £80 a week and asked who wanted it. To my utter amazement, one guy said yes, and then the other put his hand up and offered £85 a week. When you can go into a fast food restaurant and get better treatment for spending just

£5, how can a landlord or letting agent justify it when their customer is going to be spending most of their wage packet over at least six months for a bad-quality product and service? I then knew that was the level of competition I faced, and that there was a market for high-quality shared houses, which gave me confidence that I could do a whole lot better.

Analyse tenant demand

My next step was to check out tenant demand. Were there tenants out there who were willing to pay a little more for a better product and service? All it took to find out was a £50 advert in the local paper. I got 104 enquiries and I asked every single person questions. What area did they want to live in? What amenities did they want to be close to? Would they prefer a single, double or twin room? Did they want a private bathroom or en suite? What was their budget and what was most important to them, such as location or having an en suite?

I catalogued my findings in a spreadsheet and pinned the most popular locations on a map. It was a simple process that enabled me to understand my customers' needs, and it's one that anybody can follow, especially in the digital age. Look on websites such as SpareRoom. co.uk to see the number of rooms to rent in an area versus the number of tenants looking for rooms. Write down these numbers to give yourself an idea of the supply to demand ratios, but don't be put off by low ratios as there are complex factors to understand.

Back then, there was high demand and poor competition. Today, by comparison, there are a lot more investors who have cottoned on to this demand and are competing in the professional HMO market. But demand is constantly increasing (the number of tenants using SpareRoom.co.uk to find rented accommodation usually increases year on year), and good-quality HMOs are still a fantastic opportunity for investors who have the funds and motivation to succeed.

Are there any location-specific barriers?

Investing close to home will of course make the management of your properties easier and more cost-effective, and also minimise market-research time. After all, you know the area and the local amenities. Returns potential is obviously important and there are certain areas in the UK that can generate higher rental yields than others, but the likelihood is that there will be attractive investment opportunities within an hour's drive of your home.

The viability of investing near to where you live will depend on a number of factors, the most important of which is local legislation. In the case of professional-let

HMOs, two of the major things to consider are planning and licensing.

Regardless of the size of the HMO you decide to develop, it may be subject to licensing. This can even be
the case with single-occupancy buy-to-lets. Not having the right licences in place could result in hefty
fines – one couple in Uxbridge were forced to pay
£60,000 in fines for HMO licensing and management
offences in 2013,[5] and one man in Middlesbrough was
fined £6,000 in 2017 for not signing up to a compul-
sory scheme.[6]

At the time of writing, any size HMO (I'll come on to
the official definitions in a moment) needs planning
permission in Wales, and in Scotland, HMOs with
more than five people need planning permission. In
England, you may be able to create an HMO for up to
six people under permitted development rights, but
will require planning permission for seven or more
people. Where this differs is in locations which are
deemed to be over-saturated with multiple-occupan-
cy properties and there is an Article 4 (A4) Direction
in place. This removes permitted development rights,
meaning that anyone who wishes to change the use
of a property into shared accommodation for three
or more unrelated tenants must apply for planning

---

5   www.landlordzone.co.uk/news/60000-fine-couple-breaching-hmo-rules
6   www.landlordtoday.co.uk/breaking-news/2017/5/landlord-fined-6-000-for-
     not-having-hmo-licenses?source=newsticker

permission – even if any works would generally come under permitted development.

For a lot of investors, an A4 Direction would put them off. Imagine buying a house to convert to an HMO and not getting planning permission? That would be a major problem. As we're a countrywide franchise of landlords providing shared housing, the spread of A4s could have been a considerable worry for Platinum Partners, but as professional investors, we are able to adopt the sophisticated strategy of buying a property subject to planning.

One of the main reasons an area may have an A4 Direction in place is studentification. Professional HMOs are different to student HMOs, and sometimes, you just need to know how to educate the local authorities on that fact. There are some authorities, such as that in Milton Keynes, that have a militant view and often refuse everything, but this is determined by each case and is the exception, not the rule. Platinum have many partners in Oxford where the current A4 Direction is creating a shortage of affordable rooms and pushing rents above the national average.

Regardless of the type of property investment you are hoping to make, take the time to understand both the national guidelines and local authority standards, as well as other licensing and planning requirements, which can vary significantly. Do your research, starting with the planning and policy pages of your local authority's website, and make sure there is nothing stopping you from doing what you want to do.

There's no such thing as the perfect investment property

Admittedly, if you decide that the standard buy-to-let strategy is the way to go, then you will be likely to find a bigger pool of suitable properties available to buy. You'll need to be confident that there are tenants out there who will want to rent the property, but ultimately, it will come down to the numbers – how much you can buy the property for, the rent you can realistically achieve, and the running costs, including ground rent and maintenance charges on leasehold properties.

With HMOs, there's no such thing as a perfect property, but what you are looking for is specific. In most areas, there will be no more than ten properties on the market at any one time that would meet the high bar from an income point of view. Before you even start your property search, work out your numbers – the capital you have to invest, whether you're intending to get a mortgage and, if so, the LTV, the cash left over to pay for a refurbishment, and the income you'll want to generate once the property is fully tenanted. Only then will you know how many rooms you need to have in your HMO and whether you can achieve that with the properties available to buy.

Every shape and size of property could be made to work if you know what you're doing and, of course, what you're trying to achieve. Every property investor is different, and even though investing in HMOs is predominantly an income strategy, this might not be important to you with every property.

Any kind of property can work as an HMO – if you know what you're doing

And maybe it's not just the amount of income you can achieve, but the speed at which you'll be able to draw that income. In this scenario, you may not want to buy a property that will take months to convert into an HMO.

If value for money is the aim of the game, you might need to look at something that needs a lot of work, but will achieve a great uplift in development profits. Likewise, if property is expensive in your investment location and houses that would comfortably be home to six or seven tenants are hard to come by, then you may have to settle at four or five bedrooms.

There is a misconception that all HMOs have at least six lettable bedrooms. The official licensing definition is that any property housing three or more people in two or more households where facilities, such as kitchens and bathrooms, are normally shared is an HMO. This definition is used in planning, but the Use Class Order also clarifies HMOs of three to six individuals as per the C4 use class, and seven or more people in the class Sui Generis. This means that there is scope for investors with less working capital to buy a property and rent it as an HMO without doing very much work at all.

What are the pros and cons of investing in smaller HMOs vs larger HMOs?

Advantages of smaller HMOs

In theory, you could buy a three-bedroom house that could be rented to a family on the same tenancy agreement, but instead, you rent the rooms individually on different tenancy agreements and call it an HMO. This kind of property could also be cost-effectively converted into a five- or six-bedroom HMO by turning spaces such as integral garages, dining rooms and living rooms into bedrooms, as long as there is still space for a generous communal area and kitchen.

The obvious advantage with smaller HMOs, aside from them not usually needing planning permission or a licence (unless permitted development rights have been removed or additional or selective licensing is in place), is that refurbishment work would be minimal, quickly completed and cheap, allowing for the property to be tenanted and start generating an income fairly soon. They are usually easier to manage too, because fewer tenants means fewer potential problems and voids, maintenance issues, wear and tear, and neighbour complaints to deal with.

An important point to make here is that guidelines and licensing rules can change, so always aim to ensure your HMO meets the minimum standards and requirements.

The downside of smaller HMOs is the fewer rooms you have to rent out, the less rental income you are able to generate. The opportunity to add immediate value through development profits will also be reduced if you're not, on the whole, making major improvements to the property. The key is to identify properties where space can be maximised for as little cost as possible, without sacrificing quality. The number of rentable bedrooms you are able to provide will ultimately impact the profitability of the investment, and the Platinum model focuses on at least six bedrooms. Within the Platinum Property Partners network, landlords have purchased everything from Victorian terraced houses and new-build properties to bungalows and commercial buildings.

Start by looking at the immediate location. You want to avoid the most expensive house in the street because it will limit you from a comparable point of view and when it comes to future growth potential. Think about the expansion and development potential. If lots of other people have done loft conversions and/or extensions, but the current owners of the property you are viewing haven't, then the chances of getting planning permission to do so are high. You don't need to be an expert to figure something like that out.

What type of road is the property on? I went to view a property with a franchise partner in Reading and inside it was perfect, but because it was on a bend on a busy road, access via vehicles wasn't safe. As an accident hotspot, it would have been rejected by Highways for the granting of planning permission because of traffic intensification.

Internally, the most important consideration is space. Could you create the right number of bedrooms, bathrooms and communal spaces? Is there unused space under the stairs or on large landings? Room sizes are always an important factor as there are minimum bedroom and communal-space size requirements, so older properties with larger rooms may be more suitable. And even if you don't have to build, you may need to make internal structural changes to make the property more appealing to potential tenants and allow for en suites, or generally at least one bathroom for every four people (though this can vary between local authorities).

Externally, you might need space at the front of the property for off-road parking, but avoid houses with large gardens. Firstly, a small garden might mean the property is cheaper, and secondly, it needs to be low maintenance. Then, one of the key things to check, but something that a lot of novice investors overlook, is drainage. You need to be able to facilitate your additional bathrooms, so know whether you can access the drainage. It could make the difference as to whether you go ahead with the purchase or not. If it's not obvious on viewing where the access points are, ask the agent or get them to check with building control or the local water authority.

Finally, remember to check whether there are any covenants in place preventing you from doing any building work or letting the property as an HMO.

Eventually, it will come down to how much you're able to purchase the property for, the cost of the refurbishment to create the additional space and the rental income potential of the property. On the one hand, you might be able to buy a run-down property for a good price, but have to pay a high refurbishment cost to make it into a fully operational and high-quality HMO. The potential benefit of this is achieving development profits, where the improvements you make increase the capital value in the short term. On the other hand, you could pay more for a new-build property which requires little refurbishment and conversion, but there wouldn't be much opportunity to achieve a significant uplift in value.

It might be the case that you're able to work out how to cost-effectively and compliantly turn a two-bedroom terraced house into a six- or seven-bedroom HMO – you'll just need to be creative. Don't rule anything out and see as many properties as possible within a short space of time.

How to buy

There are two main ways of buying property – via estate agents (online or High Street) and at auctions. You can also buy directly from a vendor by leaflet dropping, networking, poster board or online advertising, but I wouldn't recommend this as it is a professional investment approach and not one for the faint of heart or inexperienced investor.

A lot of people think auctions are the best way to buy property, assuming the agreed price will be low because vendors are usually in a desperate situation. Most properties that come up for auction arrive there as a result of one or more of the three Ds – death, divorce and debt. Not very cheerful subjects to discuss in their own right, but they are often the reasons why properties can be purchased for lower than market value. However, the chances of finding a property that will produce fantastic returns as an HMO and you can buy it at a significant discount are rare. This is why you have to be realistic about purchase price, even at auctions.

You also need to be mindful that if you're buying an HMO, you're buying for the yield, so plan to hold the property for the long term. The number-one priority is the ROE – how much profit that house is going to make you every year as opposed to 'Can I get a really big discount off the purchase price?'. Obviously, the utopian situation is that you achieve both, but that is unlikely.

Another disadvantage of auctions is that you don't often get a good return on your time invested. The reason for this is because you have to view the property beforehand and carry out your due diligence, but when it comes to the day of the auction, you might find some unsophisticated investors just keep bidding up and putting the property out of your reach. By then, you have wasted all of that time viewing properties that you may not be able to buy. That, combined with the fact that so few properties meet the criteria for being turned into high-income-producing HMOs, makes buying at auction less than appealing. To date, fewer than 1% of properties purchased through the Platinum network have been bought at auction.

A third downside of buying at auction for the unsuspecting or inexperienced investor is the mortgageability. A property without a functioning kitchen or bathroom, for example, will not usually be mortgageable, but once you have put up your hand and the property has been granted towards you, you are committed to 10% of the purchase price and you have twenty-eight days to complete on that property. So, the risk of finding a hidden nasty can be significant.

Properties that are next to a pub or above an off licence are often quite hard to get mortgages on. Certain construction types of property, for instance those built using non-standard materials or construction methods, will have either reduced or no mortgageability, and leasehold properties with leases under a certain term length will be ruled out by some lenders.

Buying at auction can be a minefield, and if you're a novice or intermediate investor, you really need to have a professional team around you and not be committed to paying 10% of the purchase price when your hand goes up and the gavel goes bang. There are so many hidden risks in buying property at auction, but for a lot of people, this is all they do. They are good at it and know how to work the system. It's certainly an option for further into your property investment journey, but for now, the easiest way to buy at auction is to phone up the next day and ask for the list of properties that didn't sell. Now these will be back on the open market with the potential to be bought at a discount.

The most effective way to buy property is via the traditional estate agent route, and there are some tricks of the trade that will increase your chances of getting the rare unicorns of properties that come on to the market and will work as HMOs.

Operating with integrity

Success in property, as in any other business, is about building successful relationships. As I explained earlier in the chapter, one of the key reasons I wanted to invest close to home and in a concentrated location was so I could develop long-term relationships. But it's about more than just treating others with respect and being personable; it's about integrity. If you lack integrity in your business dealings, you may win in the short term, but it won't last in the long run.

Over the years I've seen people who have great drive and commitment to their business go bust because of the way they've done deals. Sometimes it's the foolishness of youth, but others believe it's clever to 'get one over' on the other party. They make a huge mistake by not appreciating the difference between sharp negotiation tactics and unethical business practices.

Property is a business where, unfortunately, most of the key professions and players involved are stereotyped as being less than straight in their business dealings. We've all heard about agents taking backhanders from investors, gazumping, gazundering, vulnerable vendors being ripped off by unscrupulous buyers... the list goes on. If you're determined to make your way as an investor, it's doubly important you can stand up to scrutiny and reassure others that you're not only serious, but trustworthy and conduct your business with integrity.

Estate agents in particular can be a bottleneck in building your property business, so you need to have them on side. Remember, they deal with time wasters every day, so give them reasons to remember you as being genuine and build a relationship with them.

Here are a few good ways to do this.

Always register face to face with an agent

First impressions count, so go in and talk to estate agents face to face. Then they can get a feel for you, and you for them. It's also worth understanding the estate agency staffing structure. You usually have trainee negotiators, junior negotiators, senior negotiators and branch managers. If I go in as a professional investor, I generally want to see a senior negotiator or branch manager so we are talking the same language.

Having said that, though, I've built some of my best agent relationships with trainees. They wanted to forge a career path and they would talk a lot, telling me many useful things about the market. They also wanted to develop a relationship with investors so would send me details before spending on advertising and putting potentially suitable properties on the open market.

Show them you're serious

Have all your information to hand when you register. You should already have your other important relationships set up: a solicitor with funds on account; mortgage broker details and an agreement in principle; proof of funds for the deposit. Any agent worth their salt will want proof of your ability to finance purchases and move quickly.

Educate them

Get to know them and explain exactly what you are looking for. Always turn up to viewings, and if the property's not right, explain why not and let the agent know what might have made it work for you. Then they will be better educated about your requirements for the future.

Know your price

Double-check your financial projections so you know where your maximum offer is, and make sure you can succinctly explain your reasoning to the agent. There are two key terms in property negotiation: your 'best offer' and your 'best and final offer'. Your best offer lets an agent know that you're close to your limit, but not at your limit; your best and final offer essentially means that's it, and there is no more. That's not to say you won't go higher, but these are the magic words to use with an agent to help them understand that this is your hard limit.

One of the advantages of using this terminology is that the estate agent will recognise you as a semi-professional/professional investor who understands the business, so remember those phrases and use them wisely.

Do what you say you're going to do

Once you've agreed a purchase, make sure you get the survey instructed as quickly as possible to show commitment, and don't reduce your offer unless the survey gives you just cause.

Differentiate yourself

Make yourself stand out with estate agents. It's common for them to congratulate you when you complete on a purchase, but why not show your appreciation for them? I used to give the agents a bottle of champagne and a card as a thank you, and then invite them to come and see the property once it was finished and the tenants were in. Then they could see for themselves what I had done and understand better the kind of thing I would be looking for next time.

In short, give agents every reason to pick up the phone to you first as soon as they value a property that might be suitable, and then recommend you to their vendor as a serious and reliable buyer. If you start messing about with the purchase price and back-tracking on negotiations, you'll quickly develop a reputation in the area and will miss out on some great opportunities. On the flip side, if you do what you say you're going to do, when you say you'll do it, you should find agents responsive over time.

CASE STUDY: THE IMPORTANCE OF REPUTATION

In 2017, a franchise partner agreed a purchase through an agent she'd viewed a number of properties with. She made sure she kept the agent updated throughout the transaction and dropped in a bottle of wine when she went to pick up the keys on completion.

Later in the year, the agent rang her about a new instruction that she thought was an absolutely ideal investment. The franchise partner viewed the property without having seen any details, knowing the agent was reliable, and made an offer. Although it was below the asking price, the agent recommended that the vendor take it, knowing she could trust that our franchise partner would complete the purchase as quickly as possible with no messing around. That's the kind of reputation to aim to build with your business.

To continue the story, the purchase of that particular property went through relatively smoothly in two months, but just before exchange of contracts, another investor suggested to our franchise partner that, as sales transactions were at low levels, she should try to negotiate £10,000 off the purchase price. She refused, saying she knew she'd already got a good deal and had shaken the vendor's hand at the agreed price, so going back on her word would be utterly wrong.

Integrity is a trait that should run through everything you do. As well as giving others faith in you, it means you'll be able to look at yourself in the mirror and know you have done the right thing, morally and ethically. Warren Buffett, arguably the world's best investor, says in one of his books, 'It takes twenty years to build a reputation and five minutes to ruin it', so never be greedy just to make an extra buck. He also says every transaction he's made seemed to be the best at the time and he never compromised his integrity in any of them. If you're looking to emulate successful people, following Warren Buffett's business principles is a good start.

I personally believe that what goes around, comes around, and in the property world there are many examples of people who haven't acted with integrity and have had their comeuppance.

CASE STUDY: KARMA IN THE PROPERTY BUSINESS

On the south coast, close to where I live, there was a developer and entrepreneur who did pretty unscrupulous deals, focusing on buying large family homes, flattening them and putting up apartment blocks, much to the disgust of local residents. This man would agree to buy a development site, and then on the day of exchange would instruct his solicitor to tell the vendor he wouldn't proceed unless they knocked anywhere from £10k to £100k off the purchase price. Those types of practices gave him a bad reputation, but he swanned about on his yacht and made no secret of the fact that if people didn't like him, he didn't care.

> Because of the money he was making, he thought he was untouchable, but when the recession started to bite in mid-2008, his main company was completely wiped out, with millions of pounds worth of debts, and he was declared personally bankrupt in October 2008.

People do business with people they like and trust. Property is first and foremost a people business, so always aim to operate with integrity from purchase right through to the management of your business.

Summary

In this chapter, we've covered:

- Carrying out competitor analysis and customer research before you decide on your investment location

- Understanding the local and national legislation in place

- Knowing your numbers before starting your property search

- Always looking to maximise the number of lettable bedrooms without compromising quality or space

- Don't rule out any property if it meets your basic online search criteria without physically viewing it

- Ensure your chosen property will meet minimum standards

- Strike up positive relationships with estate agents and always operate with integrity

CHAPTER 9

MISTAKE #6 –
BEING OVER TIME
AND OVER BUDGET

Because professionally let HMOs give such a great level of security and superb potential returns, a lot of buy-to-let investors are seeing them as a 'silver bullet' to solve their lack of cash-flow problems. Some realise they can adapt properties in their portfolios and turn them around from being cash-negative. But while it's a simple concept, it's not an easy strategy to implement correctly.

In far too many cases, investors are either unaware of the potential pitfalls or simply gloss over them, and rather than protecting their downside, they end up falling foul of the law and local council planning, building and HMO regulations. This can result in large fines, not to mention the huge costs they can incur in retrospectively ensuring a property conforms to requirements. Putting things right retrospectively is far more expensive and time consuming than getting it right first time, and sometimes it is impossible, leading to dire consequences for the investor.

Landlords who haven't been dealing with this sector for a couple of years or so are often unaware of recent and ongoing changes in legislation. There are specific ways to advertise to ensure you get the best response from prospective tenants, then managing those tenants and the property is yet another string to the HMO bow. Successfully managing an HMO portfolio is a fairly complex business, and to thrive and grow, you need to be highly professional in your approach.

Before I move into providing some practical advice on how to effectively refurbish, tenant and manage an HMO portfolio, I want to give you an idea of the tasks involved in this type of strategy. Here is a list of some of the contents from a Platinum operation manual.

PREMISES AND EQUIPMENT

Premises:
- Office space

Office equipment:
- Furniture
- Stationery
- Filing systems
- Telecommunications
- Telephones:
  - ☐ Supply of telephone services
  - ☐ 0845 numbers
- Telephone answering machine
- Fax machines
- ADSL/broadband

COMPUTER EQUIPMENT

Hardware:
- PC specification
- Printer
- Pricing

Software:
- Operating system
- Office suite
- Firewall and virus protection
- Web browser and email
- Data backup software
- Google Earth

Support/maintenance service:
- Computer
- Printer
- Data backups

VEHICLE

SUITABILITY

CLEANING AND MAINTENANCE

PROPERTY ACQUISITION

Sourcing property:
- Estate agents
- Internet
- PPP property location analyser
- Right Move/SpareRoom/ EasyRoommate etc
- Newspaper advertisement
- Responses to advertisements
- Other landlords
- PPP purchase and rental spreadsheet

Deal analysis:
- Analysing the viability of properties
- Summary of properties
- The HMO analysis tool
- Rules of thumb
- Non-mortgage funding

Viewing properties:
- Booking viewings
  - ☐ Estate agent relationships

BUYING A PROPERTY

Making an offer:
- Property analysis ratios
- Emotional detachment
- Using the correct terms

Sale agreed:
- Managing the sale
- Informing the broker
- Instructing the solicitor

- Instructing the surveyor
Property insurance
Exchange of contracts

REFURBISHMENT
Preparing properties
Standards:
- Legal and regulatory requirements
- Security services
- Décor
- Fixtures, fittings and furnishings
- Utensils and appliances
Costing projects:
- The PPP refurbishments cost sheet
Costs and economies:
- Under-spending
- Over-spending
- Property standard reviews
Planning consent and building regulations:
- Change of use
HMO licensing
Contracting the work:
- Finding good contractors
- Keeping good contractors
- Obtaining quotes
- Estimates
Payments
Project management
Site meetings:
- Changes and amendments
- Stage payments
Completions of the works:
- Sign off and snagging
- Contractor relations

TENANTS
Final arrangements:
- Utility bills
- Redirecting mail
- Lettings and management
- Marketing and letting
- Finding tenants
Marketing and advertising:
- Websites
- Word of mouth
- Existing tenants
- Estate agents/letting agents
- Local major employers
- Signboards
- Postcards in newsagents' windows
- Local hospitals
- Recruitment agencies
- Leaflet drop
- Local tradesmen
- Local business associations
Receiving enquiries:
- Call enquiry sheet
- The PPP property investment location analyser
Assessing tenants
Viewings/show-rounds:
- Personal security
- Declining enquirers
New tenants
- Taking deposits
Information packs:
- Photocopying records
References
Signing the agreement
Tenant move in:

- Inventory check
- Defects
- Keys
- Personal details

Deposit and rent payments:

- Tenancy deposit scheme
- Rent payment intervals
- Cash rent collections

Tenant administration:

- Non-payments of rents and charges
- Guests
- Personal relations with tenants
- House rules

Tenants leaving:

- Tenant gives notice to quit
- Landlord gives notice to quit
- Notes on leaving

Vacating rooms:

- Time of departure
- Room inventory check

MAXIMISING PROFITS

Cost control:

- Maximising rental income

Property administration

Repairs and maintenance:

- Repairs
- Landlords' inspections
- Local authority inspections
- Rubbish bins

Additional security

HMO licensing:

- Non-licensable HMOs
- Mandatory licensed HMOs
- Additional licensing

- HMO selective licensing

Typical requirements for HMOs

- Refurbishing

HEALTH AND SAFETY

Health and safety requirements:

- Landlord CORGI gas certificate
- Portable appliance testing (PAT)
- Landlords' five-year electrical test
- Furniture safety
- Fire inspections
- Risk assessments
- Quarterly inspections
- HMO hazards

SERVICE STANDARDS

About customers:

- Essential good practice

Office:

- Visits/show-rounds
- Taking messages
- Customer contact
- Customer care
- Keep smiling

Telephone technique:

- Golden rules
- Incoming calls
- Outgoing calls
- Telephone answering messages

Complaints:

- Dealing with complaints
- Handling a complaint

191

- Recording complaints
- Reporting complaints to head office

BUSINESS ADMINISTRATION
The business plan
Cash-flow forecast:
- Targets

Accounting and bookkeeping:
- Systems

Keeping financial records:
- Purchase invoices
- Sales invoices
- Cash book
- Petty cash
- Bank reconciliation

Stationery and telephones:
- Ordering stationery
- PPP mobile telephones

Third party suppliers

OFFICE ADMINISTRATION
Office hours
Office diary
Property record keeping:
- Filing

Electronic records:
- Tenant rent record sheet
- Rent roll and tenant information sheet
- Computer data backups

Key control:
- 'Suited keys'

Tenants vacating:
- Availability details – white board
- Office procedure following vacation

Taxation:
- Income tax
- Value added tax (VAT)

INSURANCE
Property-related insurance:
- Buildings insurance
- Contents insurance

Business-related insurance:
- Alternative accommodation and/or loss of rent
- Public liability
- Employers' liability
- Terrorism cover
- Legal expenses cover
- Landlords' tenancy legal costs
- Properties which are unoccupied for significant periods
- Landlords' rent guarantee insurance

General notes
Regular returns
Management services fee
Annual accounts
Payments and reconciliations
Staff
Confidentiality
Health and safety:
- Health and safety in the workplace
- Accident book
- HMO health and safety

Refurbishment

Having agreed a sale on a property, and understanding as much as possible about what you can do with the space and how to adhere to licensing and legislation requirements in your investment location, you need to begin the process of planning a cost-effective refurbishment.

On any property, you'll need to do a certain amount of conversion and refurbishment work to turn what is usually a family home into a high-quality HMO, but it is easy to get carried away with the aesthetics of a design rather than the practicalities and, more importantly, the legal requirements. In most cases, you will need to change existing layouts significantly to make way for additional bathrooms, larger communal spaces, extra storage facilities, and to ensure that bedrooms meet any minimum size requirements.

It makes sense for me to now hand over to Kim Thorogood, an experienced refurbishment mentor who has been supporting Platinum Property Partners for more than a decade.

Kim Thorogood: Refurbishment mentor

My role as a refurbishment mentor encompasses helping franchise partners to maximise the profitability of each particular house, do so in a compliant manner, and ensure that the tenants have a fantastic place that they can call home – with all of the required amenities and safety features.

Make sure you already know at the point of making an offer on a property that you can do what you want to do. This includes knowing how many communal spaces, bedrooms, bathrooms and en suites you want; whether the rooms will meet any minimum size requirements; if you want single or double occupancy; and what work you will require to configure the property, such as extensions, conversions, drainage work etc. For example, where are the current windows and can you move or create additional ones? This is trickier in semi-detached and terraced properties.

Then, as soon as possible (preferably before going sale agreed), you need to find out if there are any covenants or planning restrictions in place that might, for example, say you can only use the property as a single-family dwelling house or that you can't convert the garage into habitable accommodation. The latter one is particularly common. It's not a deal breaker, but you'll need to apply to get the restrictions lifted.

At this point, also check whether any work will be covered under permitted development or whether you need to get planning permission. Aim to put in any planning applications alongside the purchase process, but be aware that if, for any reason, the sale falls through, the application will belong to the vendor.

The aim of the game is to uncover any problems as soon as possible before you put together your detailed request for quotations from builders and tradespeople. Will it be a simple case of stripping wallpaper, re-skimming walls, putting in one or two en suites, replacing the kitchen and redecorating? Or do you have a bigger project on your hands? If you need to knock down walls or have Artex on your ceilings, I recommend you get an asbestos survey done.

The builders' specification should be done room by room, covering everything from checking the flow of water coming into the property and electrical and plumbing needs to what's being taken out and knocked down, what walls are going up and where, and a floor plan of where furniture is going so that the builders have the full picture.

Here's an excerpt from a specification I dealt with recently.

Convert garage to bedroom with window to front, create new access door to hallway, gas and electric meters to be moved to boxes on external wall, consumer unit to be relocated to hallway, en suite at rear of room.

That is a high-level specification, so I needed to add the detail. Below is a template I use, with examples added.

Site prelims – site clearance/skips

For example:

- Removal of old kitchen and disposal off site
- Remove built-in wardrobe from bedroom one
- Remove brick plinth from bedroom four
- Remove flooring throughout the house except tiled floor in upstairs bathroom
- Remove wallpaper from bedrooms one, two, four and hallway

Kitchen

For example:

- Wall to be removed and new partition constructed approximately 2ft back
- Serving hatch to be blocked up and wall made good
- New kitchen units to be supplied and fitted (Howdens or similar)
- Relocate electricity points to service all new appliances if necessary

Sitting room

For example:

- Partition to be constructed creating an additional room to meet building regulations requirements.

- Split light switch for new rooms (two × pendant light in sitting room, one x pendant in bedroom).

- Fit fire-retardant door to electricity meter cupboard. Ensure cupboard enclosure has 30-minute fire protection.

Dining-lounge

For example:

- Partition to be constructed dividing the room in two. Additional doorway to be created.

- Remove gas fire, cap off gas connection.

- Rear room bed two to have blown double-glazed window glazing replaced.

New ground-floor room (bedroom three)

For example:

- Create new en-suite shower room – two options (through existing door or through prior exterior wall)

- New window to patio door to replace blown glazed unit

Hall (ground and first floor)

For example:

- Fire extinguisher installed (multipurpose supplied by client). Specify as per local HMO officer requirements – fire extinguisher may not be required.

- Fire board under stairs to create 30-mins fire protection.

- Move radiator to allow for doorway to bedroom.

- Supply and fit shelf for router and Cat5e/6 Hub.

Bathroom

For example:

- Bathroom to be split by partition to create en suite to bed seven and smaller communal showroom

Airing cupboard

For example:

- Megaflo to be located here?
- Install programmer for heating

Driveway

For example:

- Dig out existing driveway and lawn, replace with permeable tarmac or block paving and landscape as specified by client. Size on the layout drawings. (Specify as applicable.)

Fencing

For example:

- Replace side fence – Waney lap with concrete posts, 6ft. Gate required next to house.

Shed

For example:

- Shed for bike storage to be sited in rear garden, 10ft × 8ft – base. (Shed to be provided by client.)

Facias, guttering, windows

For example:

- Sand down and repaint white facias
- Sand down and stain/paint windows and panels brown
- Replace any rotten facias, bargeboards

Heating, hot water and bathrooms

For example:

- Mastic sealant between sanitary ware and tiles to be mould resistant. Baths to be sealed when they are full of water.
- Isolating valves to be fitted to pipework on all taps/showers and washing machine water feed so these can be isolated for maintenance/repair.
- All radiators to be fitted with thermostatic radiator valves (TRVs).

En suites/shower rooms

For example:

- Supply and fit white shower tray, cubicle, toilet, sink and taps. Shower to be thermostatic (dependent on plumber recommendation regarding water pressure and flow to house).
- Heated towel rail in en suites connected into central heating system.
- Sink and toilet drainage to be connected to main stack.

Thermostat

For example:

- Replace heating thermostat with hardwired variable programmable controller with a locking code (tamper proof) or remote programmable (wi-fi) thermostats, eg Inspire Home Automation. Latter client to supply.

Water connections

For example:

- Ensure that wherever possible, final connections are 'hard piped'. Where this is not possible, flexible hoses should be both as short as possible, and *not* lined with ethylene propylene diene monomer (EPDM) material. All hoses must be Water Regulations Advisory Scheme (WRAS) approved.

Electrics

For example:

- Where stud walls are being put up, install TV and extra electrical sockets in walls. Where these are being added to room's current wiring, they are to be located in surface mounted trunking, running up corners of rooms where possible. (Specify if you require wiring to be chased in.)

Automatic fire detection (AFD) system

Specify as per local HMO officer requirements, for example:

- LD2 Grade D – mains wired interlinked with lithium battery backup. Smoke detectors with sounders in hallway, landings (on all floors), bedrooms, megaflo cupboard, loft, understairs cupboard, rear lobby. Heat detector with sounder in kitchen.

Or:

- Emergency lighting ground and first floor.

Sockets

For example:

- **Kitchen** – all electrics to include four double sockets above work surfaces. Plus, appropriate sockets for major appliances (cooker, dishwasher and two × fridge freezers). Specify as per your HMO officer's requirements.
- **Bedrooms/living room** – double socket × four (one socket in each room to have USB charger point).
- **Hallways:**
  - ☐ Double socket on each floor (for cleaner)
  - ☐ Double socket at high level in hallway for router

Lighting

For example:

- Pendant lights – lounge and all bedrooms
- LED spotlights – kitchen

Ventilation

For example:

- Extraction in en suites/rooms minimum 15L/min with humidity sensing control and silent running, externally vented (client to supply)

CAT 6

For example:

- CAT 6 data cabling to all bedrooms and communal room

TV points/booster

For example:

- Digital TV points in communal lounge and all bedrooms
- TV booster in loft to all TV points fitted into current aerial (or new aerial as required)

Electrics – other

For example:

- Full rewire required?
- Check the main fuse head coming into the property. This should be at least 80A, preferably 100A.
- Carbon monoxide alarm to be supplied and fitted in kitchen if gas burners are present on cooker. Also in location of boiler (if installed elsewhere). If installed in loft, link alarm into AFD.
- Electric doorbell to be fitted.

Stud walls

For example:

- Stud walls between bedrooms and en suites/shower rooms or between bedrooms and a communal area should be made as sound insulating as possible. Use sound-insulating plasterboard (blue) with Rockwool insulation between wall voids.

Decorating

For example:

- Fill in all cracks and holes prior to decoration works
- Make good plaster after installation of services and fittings (kitchen, cabling, smoke detectors, pipework etc)
- All woodwork to be sanded, undercoated where appropriate and finished in two coats of white eggshell/satinwood/gloss
- **Bathrooms** – finished in white (silk anti-fungal bathroom paint) including ceiling
- **Kitchen** – finished in silk magnolia (or desired colour if different) on walls, white silk on ceiling
- **All other rooms** – matt magnolia (or desired colour if different) on walls, white ceilings
- All radiators white

Flooring

For example:

- **Carpet** – Gala Berber Fallen Leaf (or preferred colour) felt-backed carpet with a good acoustic underlay for bedrooms, stairs, first-floor landing. Please provide cost for supply and fit, and advise supply price per metre.
- **Vinyl floor Polyflor** – (colour to be confirmed) for hall, kitchen/communal area, shower rooms, en suites.

Other:

- Fit curtain poles/blinds, mirrors, picture hooks and door numbers (client to supply)
- Install rotary washing line (client to supply)

- Fit TV bracket to wall in communal area (client to supply)

As the list above shows, you will have a considerable amount of work to do, and this is just a high-level summary.

With regards to fire safety specifically, all landlords have legal obligations to comply, but different legislation applies to different kinds of rented accommodation. HMOs will require far higher levels of fire safety regulation than other residential properties. Minimum requirements might just be a fire door in the kitchen, a smoke detector in the hallway and on the landing in a two-storey property, and escape windows from bedrooms. At the other end of the spectrum, you may need fire doors on all bedrooms, the living room, cupboards in hallways, and an LD1 Grade A fire alarm system which has a control panel with breakable glass call points on all floors and smoke detectors in all bedrooms, on the landings, in the loft space and basement, and a heat detector in the kitchen.

When it comes to finding a builder, get at least three quotes and always meet the builder at the property to talk through the work required. A personal recommendation is great, but their track record and credentials are more important.

Almost all refurbishment work associated with an HMO conversion must comply with building regulations, which can be interpreted and signed off by both a local authority and private approved inspector. This applies to everything from window installation, sound insulation, and gas and electrical safety to ventilation, sanitation and drainage, fire alarms, and emergency lighting.

All building work must also comply with construction, design and management (CDM) regulations. This is why it is crucial to use reputable contractors (preferably members of a trade association) who have the relevant experience and qualifications. Prior to being let, for example, all rental properties must be electrically tested by a qualified electrician, and PAT must be carried out annually. An annual gas safety check must also be carried out by a Gas Safe registered engineer and records provided to tenants within twenty-eight days of the work being completed, and to new tenants when they move in.

In addition, you need to decide whether you are going to manage the project or get the builder to do it for you. The former is cheaper, but the latter is a great way to learn and will be money well spent. Whatever you do, get a schedule of works from the builder, outlining how long the project is likely to take and what they're going to do and when. It also helps with payments, so you can ensure you only pay for complete works and are able to arrange carpet and furniture delivery, for instance.

In terms of how much to budget for an HMO refurbishment, well... how long is a piece of string? It depends on how much you buy the property for, what work needs to be done, and whether the achievable rental income and potential for development profits will make it a good ROI. One thing I will say is that it's easy to go over budget, especially first time round. And there are several reasons for this.

Firstly, if you haven't listed everything down that you want to do, or you change your mind during the project, this can have a costly impact. Secondly, you can spend a lot of time rectifying costly mistakes, which is why preparation and picking the right builder are so important. No matter how organised you are, you can never be 100% sure that you won't find any hidden nasties, so always add a 10% contingency, at least, to your budget for what you can't see until you start pulling the property apart.

Thirdly, keep reminding yourself that you are not going to be living in the HMO. It's not about what you would want in the house or how you would refurbish or redecorate it; it's about creating a high-quality and safe environment for tenants to live in, but in a cost-effective way. This is a business after all.

And last but not least, make sure you're covered – properties require certain insurance policies when undergoing refurbishment.

I hope these insights and the benefit of Kim's experience have been helpful for you.

One other thing I would like to add here, and it goes back to operating with integrity, is that it's bad business practice to take several months to settle suppliers' invoices. This goes for refurbishment as well as ongoing property management and maintenance. It shows a lack of organisation, professionalism or cash flow, and ultimately brings your trustworthiness into question. Nobody wants to do business with people they can't trust.

As a property investor, you tend to deal with lots of small businesses and sole traders, who often live month-to-month, so make sure you pay them as soon as possible. They are also usually the tradespeople you or your property manager will need to call on at short notice, and they're far more likely to move quickly to fix problems if they know you always pay on time.

Ready to rent

Kim has highlighted how the practical elements of a refurbishment are much more important in the first instance than making your property look pretty, but this is still important.

The number-one rule for HMO interior design is to keep it simple, neutral and nice. Always bear in mind that you're not going to live in the property and what you like isn't necessarily what your tenants will like, or need. Having said that, the quality of the finish and furnishings could affect how much rent you are able to charge. Always think about your target tenant and what it will take to make them feel at home.

You don't have to paint the whole house in magnolia, but make sure you opt for a neutral colour that will always be in stock for touch-ups and go with any colour scheme. This will also make it easier to replace furniture without the need to match a distinctive gloss or matt. Use anti-mould paint in the kitchen and bathroom, and anywhere else that might be exposed to dampness.

Never opt for the cheapest range of furniture available as it will cost you more in the long run for repairs and replacement. Purchasing as much furniture from one supplier as possible will mean you can achieve big savings, but make sure it comes with a warranty. Easy-to-clean material, such as leather or 'pleather' for sofas, is a good idea.

Tiles, hardwood and laminate flooring look nice and avoid the constant use of carpet cleaner, but can make the house noisy and cold if you use them throughout. They're necessary in the bathrooms and communal areas, but use a durable patterned or mottled carpet in the rest of the house. Greys, browns and beiges go with almost anything, and more importantly, hide stains well.

A fully equipped kitchen is essential, of course, as is providing a television in the communal area if you want happy tenants, but it's often a strong broadband connection that makes the difference. Storage, sometimes specific areas for each tenant, is also important. This includes in the bedrooms as well as the kitchen, and in some instances, outside storage for bikes.

Here are some pictures of Platinum HMOs.

Finding the right tenants

At this point, you have been spending money left, right and centre, and it can be a scary experience, so as soon as you're ready to welcome rent-paying tenants, make sure you do everything you can to find the right ones.

Firstly, finding tenants who want to live in shared accommodation often requires the use of different resources to tenanting a single-occupancy property. As well as traditional advertising channels, such as SpareRoom.co.uk, utilise free resources as much as possible, like Gumtree or social media platforms. Think about where your potential tenants 'hang out' and spend time. So many franchise partners are seeing great results through social media, and some are building relationships with big employers who often fund relocations and the like.

When you start getting enquiries, it's then a case of selecting the right tenant. For an HMO, it's about much more than right to rent, identity, income, employment and referencing checks, to name just a few. While someone might pass the test on paper, they may not be a good fit with the other housemates, and that can cause you major issues. It's a personal process, and as a result, quite time consuming.

In addition to doing the official referencing checks, get to know your prospective tenant. Call them to ensure they meet your primary criteria – this could include age, gender and interests, depending on the current tenants in situ. Can you have a conversation with them and do they seem genuine?

Find out if they have lived in a house share before and what their previous housemates were like, and clarify details of your house and location. Often those looking to share are new to the area and may not realise how far the property is from their workplace, so you have a moral obligation to be honest with them. Then conduct the viewing when at least some of the other housemates are at home so you can introduce the prospective tenant and see if they are likely to get along. Explain the house rules and expectations so neither you nor the prospective tenants get any nasty surprises.

Franchise partner and award-winning landlord, Gertie Owen, loves the people side of her property business and is known for her extra special treatment of tenants, or housemates as she likes to call them. She'll never turn up to a viewing looking less than her best as she believes, and rightly so, that first impressions are important. Gertie always goes out of her way to pick potential housemates up from the station for a viewing if they don't drive and makes sure she shows them around the area, especially if they aren't local. The property itself will be immaculate, and at Christmas or Easter, her housemates will get gifts.

It's not always an option to operate in this way, but it's certainly worked for Gertie. She consistently gets five-star feedback.

Avoiding voids – effective property management

The great thing about investing in HMOs is that it's highly unlikely you'll experience a 100% void in your property. Letting multiple rooms on an individual basis means that even when one or two tenants move out, the property is still generating a rental income. But the more tenants you have, the harder it is to manage them, and you want to avoid having to fill a room in your property every month, which costs time and money.

In the first instance, minimise the potential of having a void by keeping good long-term tenants happy. You can do this by:

- Responding to any tenant or maintenance problem quickly, even if you think it's unjustified

- Being flexible and responsive to specific requests, such as when a good tenant asks to have a friend to stay or put a picture up

- Maintaining the property to a high standard inside and out, and perhaps employing a cleaner and/or gardener

- Thinking carefully before you consider a rent increase

When you find yourself in the position of having to find replacement tenants:

- Advertise as soon as your current tenant gives notice

- Review the rent to ensure it is set at the right rate for what you are offering and in line with market rents

- Add value by setting expectations, such as explaining additional benefits like a cleaner and all-inclusive bills

- Select tenants that you know will be happy in your house and with existing housemates

- Be organised so that when you do have a new tenant interested, everything is ready

Of course, it may not be your intention to be hands-on in the day-to-day management of tenants. Initially, I would advise against using a property manager, so you get to understand how the business runs and set some guidelines for how you want your portfolio to be managed. In the long run, though, when you're ready and want to take a step back and enjoy the passive benefits of having a profitable buy-to-let property portfolio, you can get someone else to take over the reins, but be mindful that a study by SpareRoom.co.uk found that 87% of tenants prefer to deal directly with a landlord. This begs the question – how can you keep your tenants happy while freeing up more of your own time?

One alternative to a letting agent is to consider hiring the help of a property manager. This way, you can not only avoid hefty management fees by setting your own competitive rates of pay, but also pick the right person for you and, more importantly, your brand.

All that said, ask yourself these three important questions to determine whether you are ready for a property manager, mentally and financially.

Can you afford to hire a property manager?

If you've been running your buy-to-let portfolio effectively as a business, then you should be able to accurately assess your financial returns and work out whether you can afford the additional expense of hired help. Is this money you want to part with in return for some freedom? Again, we're back to understanding your numbers and knowing what your goals are.

To do this, you'll need to evaluate how much time you actually spend on managing the portfolio yourself to determine how many hours a week a property and lettings manager will need to work. A good way to do this is to track your activity over a short period.

Are you prepared to hand over control?

After running things your own way, you might find it hard to hand over control. Property managers can relieve you of 100% of the running of your property business, which involves them having access to bank accounts and personal records, or they could start off by taking over certain aspects such as finding tenants and conducting viewings. Establish what you feel comfortable with, and perhaps try hiring someone for some of the work to see how you feel.

Do you want to manage staff?

Hiring a property manager comes with a long list of responsibilities. Even if you are used to managing staff from current or previous roles, are you ready to hire, fire, discipline and appraise again? You'll need to consider what you pay them and how, what training you will give and when, and establish performance targets. Also, will the property manager be self-employed or employed? The latter will make you vulnerable to a whole host of additional regulations.

It might sound as though I'm trying to put you off, and in a way, I suppose I am. Unless you've looked at all the potential downsides to operating this business model and are certain you can deal with them effectively, you'd probably be better not taking this path. But if you are sure, please be reassured that with the right advice and support, there are solutions to nearly all challenges.

Summary

In this chapter, we've covered:

- Not underestimating the complexity of the HMO model

- Focusing on compliance before aesthetics when it comes to refurbishment

- Appointing a good team around you and having a schedule of works

- Thinking about what your tenants want and need rather than your own preferences

- Taking time to find the 'right' tenant

Remember that effective property management is the key to minimising voids.

CHAPTER 10

MISTAKE #7 – NOT DEVELOPING PARTNERSHIPS

I have studied success, both personally and professionally, for the past thirty years, and I have distilled down what makes people successful in terms of wealth, health and happiness into one simple core principle and three powerful sub-principles.

My core success principle is **partnerships**. There are lots of different kinds of partnerships, so if you want to learn more about my thinking on this critically important topic, please visit my website – www.stevebolton. com – and/or join my private Facebook group – www. facebook.com/stevebolton99. There is no such thing as 'self-made success'; we all need help.

My three sub-principles for success are:

- Stand on the shoulders of giants
- Invest in yourself
- Expand and upgrade your network

I'll now explain these in more detail.

Stand on the shoulders of giants

Simply put, standing on the shoulders of giants is a concept based around mentoring. I believe that everybody should have mentors. A mentor is someone who has been there and done it, and often faced many failures and setbacks along the way before achieving the types of results that you are looking to replicate.

Mentors, coaches and training all assist you in your development, but you need to be clear on the differences between them – the roles they play and their skillsets. These brief descriptions should help.

Coaching

The Chartered Institute of Personnel and Development defines coaching as developing a person's skills and knowledge so that their job performance improves, hopefully leading to the achievement of organisational objectives. It may also have an impact on an individual's private life. Coaching usually lasts for a short period and focuses on specific skills and goals.

A coach has a skillset that's about helping you find the best solutions to challenges and problems you've got, but they won't actually have gone out and done what you want to do. Coaches help you establish which areas of your life are out of balance and what obstacles are blocking your path to success, and work with you to move you forward in your life and business much more effectively. They challenge your thinking and make you answerable to them, which is a great motivator for achieving the goals you set together. And because a coach is generally someone from outside your business and social circle, they can be completely objective about what changes you need to make.

You could have a coach for your property investing business who knows little about property investing, but is great at identifying and helping you work on areas of weakness.

Mentoring

Mentoring is traditionally associated with an experienced person guiding and passing on their knowledge to others. The mentee could be following in their mentor's footsteps or using them as a role model, but the modern twist to this is the reverse mentoring process.

This is a relationship in which a younger person has experience that they can share with the older generation – such as information technology. Essentially, mentoring is about sharing knowledge and experience.

A mentor is someone who has been through the school of hard knocks and achieved success in a way that you would like to replicate. In the case of property investment, they will have made and lost money, probably several times, worked out robust strategies and systems, tried numerous financing strategies and mastered the best, and have a solid portfolio which brings them income and provides long-term financial security.

Training

Training is used when a skill – whether situational, theoretical or practical – needs to be taught. Examples of training-related activities include using new IT software, learning how to negotiate or how to do effective bookkeeping. The trainer teaches the information in a prescriptive mode.

I am where I am today largely because of the mentors and coaches I have had over the years. There's no way I would have been able to accelerate my success in the way I have without their training, guidance and support, and I'm continually looking for people who can improve me and my businesses. I've worked with some high achievers – Olympic gold medallists, billionaires, successful property investors – and one thing all these men and women have in common is that they are lifelong students. Whatever level they've reached, they know they can always improve and that there is something new to learn every day. Franchise partner, legendary athlete and someone I mentor, Kriss Akabusi, is a perfect example.

Don't be complacent and sit back, simply believing what you see and hear from supposedly reliable sources. Do your due diligence, question the information and be prepared to learn something that challenges what you might have believed up until that point.

Invest in yourself

'The best investment you can make is in yourself.'
— Warren Buffett

This is an investment that can't be taxed, and not even inflation can take it away from you. The more we learn, the more we earn, and as we are all, to a greater or lesser degree, unconsciously incompetent in certain areas of business and life, we can't excel in something if we stop learning, no matter how much we *think* we know about a subject.

There are many ways to tap into this knowledge – books,

training workshops, linking up with business partners – but for me, the Holy Grail of learning is simple: choose partners and mentors who have been there and done it. It's worked for me in my past, and I've been recommending the same for others for many years now.

If you've ever read autobiographies of successful people, you will know that they've had people to help them along the way. Even the world's greats have mentors – Ed Roberts mentored Bill Gates, Steve Jobs mentored Mark Zuckerberg, and Elton John mentored Ed Sheeran. The list goes on and on.

I'm a great believer in the Occam's Razor principle, that the simpler solutions are more likely to be correct than the more complex ones, which can be expanded and applied to business like this. you have the greatest chance of success in the fastest time if you follow a model that you know works and learn from those who have already trodden the path. Stand on the shoulders of giants and take advantage of the wonderful opportunity you have to avoid making the mistakes others have made.

For some people, ego and pride get in the way. This is generally truer for men than for women, for the same reason most men don't like to ask for directions when they get lost, but it only makes sense if you are happy being on a slow path to success, as opposed to the fast-track.

Don't underestimate the importance of learning your strategies from people who have proven they know how to achieve the same things you want to achieve. Nobody gets things right first time – and rarely second or third time. Why wouldn't you take advantage of someone else's experience, benefiting from them having already made and learned from the mistakes? It's a short-cut to success and by far the smartest way forward.

The average millionaire is said to have lost most of their money around three times before they find a way to hold on to it. Why choose to go that route yourself when there are now so many opportunities to access refined and proven strategies? Buying a property is not difficult – any idiot can do it – but buying a property that will meet and deliver on your financial objective – whether that's high capital growth and/or great income – is a science.

Edgar Dale's Cone of Experience illustrates how effectively we absorb and retain information, ie learn. His research showed that the more actively engaged our senses are, the more likely we are to remember something, so books, DVDs and audio learning tools are only going to be a fraction as effective, long term, as physically experiencing and being involved in whatever we want to learn.

Here is a simplified version of Dale's original cone, first published in 1946 in his book *Audiovisual Methods in Teaching*:

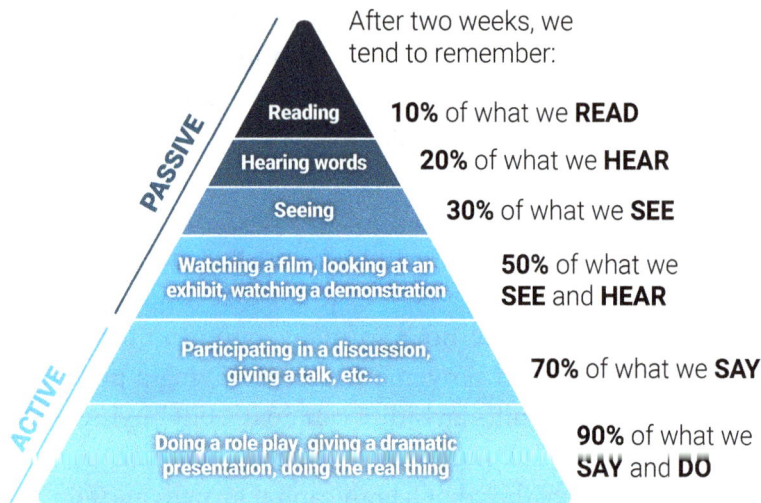

As the cone illustrates, there's huge value in physically going out there and working alongside successful property entrepreneurs and businesspeople. I can give you the names of people I believe are the best at what they do, and at the back of this book I've included a list of materials you're likely to get a lot out of, but ultimately you need to find coaches and mentors whose personality and style fit with yours.

Expand and upgrade your network

Once you surround yourself with successful people, by adopting their attitude and approach, and following their core business principles, you'll become more successful yourself. I guarantee it. I was at a point in my life, about twenty years ago, when I suddenly realised that I was pretty much the most successful person in my social circle, and I wasn't moving forward at the same rate I had been.

> 'Your network equals your net worth.'
> — Mark Victor Hansen

This quote is absolutely true. A key contributing factor to the amount of wealth you'll create is to surround yourself with successful people. A good metaphor is a cold tap dripping into a warm basin – the cold droplet is absorbed and the temperature of it raised by the warmth of the larger quantity of warm water. Similarly, a hot drip going into a cold basin will be cooled quickly. If you want to become more like other successful people, you need to have as warm a basin as possible – ie a network which is more successful and wealthier than you and will constantly raise your success temperature.

> 'If you're the smartest person in the room, you're in the wrong room.'
> — Harvey Smith

If you want to gain access to the best deals and be able to move quickly and effectively in property investing, you need your 'power team' to be 100% behind you. You need to understand what your strengths are and surround yourself with other experts who can help you develop your areas of weakness. In property specifically, you might need support on the legal and financial side, for example.

> 'You're the average of the five people you spend the most time with.'
> — Jim Rohn

In recent years, I've started to challenge this saying in its exact form because who in their right mind would cast aside their children, spouses and close friends just because they aren't wealthier or more successful than they are? Factors like your past experience, level of motivation, qualifications and skills also have an impact on the results you generate in life. In a professional capacity, it's truer to say you're *more likely* to become like the people you spend most time with.

For example, think of a time where you have been surrounded by negative people who are complaining. Does that make you feel good or bad? The latter, I'd imagine. Conversely, think about a time when you've been around inspiring, fun, positive and supportive people. It's obvious that people we spend a lot of time with do have a significant impact on us, so choose carefully.

There are great communities on the internet these days, but in my experience, nothing is as powerful as real-time face-to-face contact, mentoring and mutually aligned long-term relationships. But it isn't an either/or situation and I would encourage you to utilise both. If you haven't done so already, please apply to join my free virtual partner network on Facebook – www.facebook.com/stevebolton99.

Find people who have achieved the type of success you desire for yourself. These people may be businesspeople and entrepreneurs you already know personally, or they may be people you simply know by reputation and admire. Talk to them; ask them questions about significant points in their life and how they approached and handled certain situations. What businesses are they in? What works, what doesn't? It's only by understanding exactly how someone achieved something that you can hope to replicate that success.

Don't be afraid to approach anyone to ask for guidance. Most people in the world want to help and give, so it may surprise you what you can get if you just ask. Many successful people, when they're told something is impossible or they can't do it, refuse to accept that. Instead, they challenge it. That's how you need to think if you want to make the most out of every opportunity.

If you aren't able to invest in your personal and professional development financially, think about what else you have to offer in return. Bartering is the oldest form of purchasing, so go into every contact situation with a creative win-win attitude. Although you will certainly need to invest money somewhere along the line to accelerate your success, you can get some invaluable experience, skills and insight into the patterns that lead to long-term wealth for an investment of your time and an exchange of knowledge. It all takes effort, but the time investment you make in your own development will pay dividends in the long term.

And don't make the mistake of thinking there is one amazing person out there who will give you everything you need. You get little nuggets of gold from different people with different skills and experiences.

Whom can you trust?

If you can't trust what you read in the papers, and you don't rely solely on friends, family or acquaintances to buoy you up, where do you get advice from and whom do you trust? Rather than making the mistake of believing what you're told by people already around you, try actively seeking out success.

The first step is to identify some key people whose success, lifestyle and approach you admire. If possible, and if you know them, spend more time with these people. Be curious and ask questions and see how you might be able to help them in return.

If the person you admire has a public profile, then read the books they have written and those they recommend; watch inspirational and motivational DVDs; and go on carefully selected, recommended courses. You can even go into business with people to learn from them how to do business. Some of my best mentors have actually been business partners – they're not famous people; they've just been inspirational in terms of what they have achieved.

Summary

In this chapter, we've covered:

- Identifying people whose success and lifestyle you want to replicate

- Standing on the shoulders of giants and learning from those who have been there and done that

- Investing in yourself and never ceasing to learn

- Expanding and upgrading your network and surrounding yourself with the right people

PART THREE
CONCLUSION

CHAPTER 11
MOTIVATION

Be motivated towards success

Following my partnership principle and the three sub-principles is important, but it has to be driven by a motivation to achieve results. You can understand those three principles theoretically and conceptually, but if you don't have the motivation and drive to make some changes in your life, then nothing will happen. It's the difference between self-help and shelf-help.

There are a number of things that you can do to get motivated, and if this is an area you struggle with, I will give you some quick pointers here. But ultimately, I would recommend going online and watching some videos or buying some books about motivation.

There is a range of tools, tricks and techniques that can help you.

At a simplistic level, motivation is driven by two things: pain and pleasure. And ideally, you want to use both of those things to good effect to help you move forward. Put another way, it's the carrot and stick approach.

Think about the consequences of you not making a change. Think about the negative impact a year from now, two years from now and beyond if you don't make choices and take action around your financial future. What will the impact be on your family and others around you? What will your retirement look like?

Pain is much easier to use as motivation if a change has been forced upon you. Take redundancy, for example. Whenever someone tells me they've been made redundant, the first thing I say is 'Congratulations'. It's an unforeseen opportunity to take stock, pause, reflect and decide if now is the time to create a different future – a more exciting and fulfilling future that could take you on a journey towards financial independence.

Conversely, you also want to use pleasure. Focus on the benefits of what any change, like building your own property portfolio, will have on your life. Think about how many more choices you will have.

Most people talk about property as providing them with a secure pension, but do you really want to wait until you've retired to enjoy spending time and money doing something other than the daily grind? Why wait until your twilight years to do the things you actually want to do?

One of the most important personality traits in all successful businesspeople is optimism – a belief that anything is possible, combined with a drive to work hard and never give up. A lot of people carry with them a belief that there is something negative about having a lot of money; that success in business implies too much personal sacrifice and a cut-throat attitude; and that while others might have wealth, they're probably not happy.

In my life, I was driven by the pain of failure and the pleasure of having choices. I've chosen to take an average of three months' holiday a year to travel the world with my wife and children; I have a boat I regularly take out in the afternoons (rain or shine) to go fishing with friends; I go skiing with my mates, to sporting events with my kids, and have the time to concentrate on my own personal fitness and wellbeing. I'm happy. I give to and support charities, and one of my greatest rewards in life is seeing people I've mentored achieve their desired quality of life, knowing I've helped them on their way. I'm saying all this not to impress you, but to impress *upon you* what is possible. Remember,

I left school at sixteen with no qualifications and low self-confidence; I also lost everything I had at one point and had to start all over again. If I can create the life I want to live, then I truly believe you can too.

People say money can't buy you happiness, but that's not strictly true. Money might not be able to buy friends or love, but it can give you a great deal of security, more choices and more freedom. Wealthy people can afford to give their children a lot of opportunities in life – they can have music lessons and sports coaching; they can visit different countries and experience different cultures; if they're sick, they can receive the best medical care; they attend the best schools and live in a lovely home.

Ask yourself this question: would you rather be poor and happy or rich and happy? Happiness and wealth are not mutually exclusive. When faced with this kind of 'either/or' choice, most people will choose both – happy *and* rich.

By now, you may well feel buoyed up with ideas and good intentions, and promise yourself you're going to go away and take positive steps, but it's completely natural to find them harder to carry out as time goes on. You're used to using your time in a particular way and prioritising certain tasks over others, and habits are hard to break. This is where so many people fall down, and unless you make a concerted effort to change and improve how you approach your goals and the challenges and obstacles in your life, you'll never be as successful as you could be.

One of the best ways to make sure you follow through with your good intentions is to make yourself accountable to someone. When people ask whether Platinum Partners give any guarantees the systems and methods we use will work for them, the answer is always no. I know the systems work – they're tried, tested and proven – but the vital variable is the person operating the model.

Where you are in your life today is a direct reflection on how you've been operating in your personal and business life up until now. This means that if you're not as happy, successful, wealthy, healthy, fulfilled, etc as you would like to be, then something fundamental needs to change.

I cannot stress enough how important this is: don't make the mistake of not investing in your personal and professional development. If you follow that advice, the fruits of this investment will be with you for the rest of your life and you'll be setting a great example to your children and/or other family members. If, for whatever reason, you don't invest in a coach or mentor, it's up to you to make sure you really work on motivating yourself so that you don't fall into analysis paralysis.

What's stopping you?

People suffer from analysis paralysis in all walks of life, but you don't always see signs to identify it. When you're talking about property investment, though, the signs are much easier to spot. This is especially true at networking events – the people suffering from analysis paralysis are those listening intently to every free seminar they can find, scribbling pages upon pages of notes, and accumulating a huge stash of literature in a carrier bag – the 'shelf-help' brigade I referred to earlier. They're knowledgeable, love talking about property, have usually paid quite a bit of money for DVD sets and weekend courses, and will ask lots of questions. But, in almost every case, when you ask whether they've got any investments, the answer will be no. Usually, they're 'about to' and 'just trying to decide on the right opportunity'.

If that sounds like you, smile at yourself and read on. You're not alone – we've all suffered from analysis paralysis at some point. The main reason why people have this mental block preventing them from taking action is fear of failure. Analysis paralysis is procrastination: putting off taking the leap because of fear of choosing the wrong investment route and/or losing money, and it goes back primarily to their attitude towards risk. Someone who's risk-averse is likely to have a serious case of analysis paralysis, whereas someone who's more optimistic and action-oriented probably won't.

If you are naturally cautious, don't push yourself too far out of your comfort zone because you've seen the pound signs and think you should go for the opportunity that offers the biggest rewards. Chances are it'll come with the highest risk too. Pick something that's a little more secure, even if it offers lower returns. You don't want to spend the next few years constantly worrying about whether you're going to lose all your savings. Using property to make money is about improving your quality of life; it shouldn't be a headache.

Property, when done in the right way, defies the typical risk-analysis dynamics. High-return investments are usually considered to be high risk, but using the professional-let HMO strategy, you are able to generate high, consistent and stable returns in a low-risk manner.

How long have you been thinking about professional property investment?

When did you first start seriously looking at the options available to you? If the answer is more than a year ago and you still haven't actually invested in expanding your portfolio or moving into a highly cash-flow-positive strategy, it's time to address why that is, and the first step is a reality check.

Do you wish you'd made the move five or even ten years ago? I certainly wish I'd got into property in a much bigger way back in the mid-nineties, because if I had, I know I'd have been able to ride the storm that hit me as a result of 9/11 and the Foot-and-mouth disease, and wouldn't have had to liquidate my business and sell my home. Hindsight is a great thing, and we can all wish we'd done things differently, but none of us has a time machine to go back, nor does time wait for us. Get over your regrets and appreciate that the future is uncertain.

Of course, there are periods when the market is going up and when it's going down, but you can win in both markets, benefiting from good capital growth in boom periods and being able to negotiate hard and get great discounts when it's busting. Forget worrying about the 'when' and concentrate on the 'why' and the 'what'.

There are lots of good investments out there, and now and then you'll come across a great one. If you're too focused on finding the absolute best, the truth is you probably never will. Over-analysis, driven by the fear of making a mistake, is what's preventing you from progressing, so take a step back and reassess what's actually motivating you to make this investment and what you need from it in terms of financial return. That should enable you to discount certain types of opportunities and leave you with a shortlist.

If you look at the decision-making process and break it down, you'll find it ultimately comes down to pain and pleasure. People will make a decision and take action more often and more quickly when they're driven by pain, so if pain causes a change in behaviour while pleasure tends to sustain it, it follows that if you're relatively happy with your life and have no real catalyst for change, you're less likely to take a leap into a new field. That could be at the root of your lack of commitment to moving forward. You need to really think about what will happen if you don't make the step to invest. If things are OK for you now, think five to twenty years into the future and examine the longer-term consequences of not changing. For example, is your current pension provision going to be enough and what future commitments might you have?

What other wealth-creation options are available to you?

You may have an idea of where you want to be financially five or ten years from now, but many people don't. One of the first things to do is to understand where you are financially, and where you're trying to get to. At Platinum Property Partners, before people are approved to join the network, we create an accurate and minimum ten-year business plan and financial P&L forecast with them. This helps us and them to understand exactly what they are aiming for over what timeframe and how it should play out in a financial sense. Having this roadmap is absolutely critical.

Only by understanding your finances can you ask yourself what alternatives to property investment are likely to provide you with the kind of rewards you're looking for. In my experience, there's nothing that can rival property as a secure money-making vehicle, offering anywhere near the same level of security, capital growth and income-generating potential.

If your original motivation for getting into property investment was that you weren't where you'd hoped you'd be by now, and even after everything you've read, you're still unsure about making your move, make a copy of this next statement and stick it somewhere you can't miss it.

If the path you've taken up until now hasn't provided you with the financial security or independence you've been looking for, then maybe now is the right time to take some positive steps and make your move. You are never too old or too young.

And if you think you are too old, be inspired by the story of Colonel Harland Sanders. Whether you like KFC or not, this story is truly amazing and inspirational because it's an example of how perseverance, dedication and ambition, along with hard work, can create success, regardless of your age.

Colonel Harland Sanders has become a world-known figure by marketing his 'finger lickin' good' Kentucky fried chicken. One of the most amazing aspects of his life is the fact that when he reached the age of sixty-five, after running a restaurant for several years, he found himself penniless. He retired and received his first social security cheque for $105. And that was just the beginning of his international fame and financial success story.

With little means at his disposal, Colonel Sanders travelled door to door to houses and restaurants all over his local area, wanting to partner with someone to help promote his chicken recipe. Needless to say, he wasn't met with enthusiasm. He then travelled by car to different restaurants and cooked his fried chicken on the spot for restaurant owners. If the owner liked the chicken, they would enter into a handshake agreement to sell it. Legend has it that Colonel Sanders heard 1,009 nos before he heard his first yes.

OK, let me repeat that. He was turned down *one-thousand and nine* times before his chicken was accepted once.

The deal was that for each piece of chicken the restaurant sold, Sanders would receive a nickel. The restaurant would receive packets of his secret herbs and spices in order to avoid them knowing the recipe. By 1964, Colonel Sanders had 600 franchises selling his trademark chicken. At this time, he sold his company for $2 million dollars, but remained as a spokesperson. In 1976, Sanders was ranked as the world's second most recognisable celebrity. It's amazing how the man started at the age of sixty-five, when most retire, and built a global empire out of fried chicken.

Believe. Dream. Try. Succeed. Age is no bar.

Summary

In this chapter, we've covered:

- Using pain and pleasure to motivate you towards success

- Not falling into the analysis paralysis trap

- The need to take action

CHAPTER 12
TAKING ACTION

Property is an exciting and rewarding business. It can also be a lot of hard work if you do it all yourself. As a passive investor, you have little or no work to do beyond finding the right partners and investments. If you choose to be an active investor and build your investment portfolio in a hands-on way, you need to have a wide skill base and be able to multi-task.

In Chapter 3, I talked about goals. If you aren't already thinking about them, here's a recap and some more points for you to consider.

Ideas, goals, decisions

Ideas are things you might like to be, do, have or give in life. Goals, you are more serious about. Decisions are firm commitments you are acting on.

I like to say that goal setting doesn't work. What I mean by that is the things you achieve in life are the things you have made firm commitments towards, so you make them happen. But having a list of ideas, goals and decisions is powerful because you can move items between these lists as you see fit. And be clear on what you might like compared to what you will make happen. Ideally, come up with a list of ideas, goals and decisions on goals for the next quarter, the next year, and the next three years.

Human beings are goal-oriented creatures, and everybody has goals whether you write them down or not. Every time you do something, you're working towards an objective. When it comes to property investing, you might not necessarily be able to say what property goals you want to achieve in certain time-frames because you don't know what you don't know, so start with your lifestyle goals.

Probably the easiest to specify are your lifestyle goals for the next three to twelve months, but they'll depend on what you ultimately want to achieve long term, so picture your ideal future. Whether you do a vision board – putting images on a piece of paper as a visual representation of your goals – a list or a spreadsheet, choose a format that works for you and decide what you want to create in your life. Do you want to work forty-eight weeks a year and have four weeks' holiday, or do you want to take three months' holiday? Would you like to work three weeks and then take a week off, or would you like to work six months on and six months off? What places do you want to travel to; what contribution do you want to make to the world; what material possessions do you aspire to have; what do you want for your family and friends…? Don't be afraid to think big. It's a fact that we tend to overestimate our short-term goals and underestimate our long-term goals, so make those five- and ten-year plans something to get excited about.

Once you have your ideal future, break it down. The pattern you want and the way you choose to balance work and home life will affect what direction you pursue in your property business, because time off is reliant on leveraged income. Whether that's achieved by employing staff to take care of the daily running of your portfolio when you're not there or choosing to invest in purely passive opportunities is up to you. It will also be dependent on the amount of initial capital you have and whether your primary focus is on having monthly income or lump-sum capital returns. But start with what you *want*, not with what you currently *have*; don't limit your goals by focusing on what you believe is achievable based on your situation today.

A Platinum franchise partner has monthly, three-monthly, one-year and five-year goals, primarily focused on his financial position, portfolio size and structure, and time management, which he updates monthly. Another has monthly, one-year, three-year and five-year goals.

Here are some highlights from their recent updates:

Primary aim:

- To become financially independent and not have to rely on employed income
- To have a minimum of £120k leveraged income per annum
- To have robust and secure pension provision
- To have time, money and location freedom
- To have a minimum of £1 million trust fund and financial legacy for my children

Five-year objectives:

- I will have £2.5 million of property assets with £1 million of equity

- I will generate a leveraged income of £120k per annum

- I will be able to choose when I work and what kind of work I take on

- I will only work with people I like and trust

- I will exercise three times a week and be in the best physical and mental shape of my life

- I will have a second home in France

- I will have a great relationship with my wife and kids

- I will own my own sailing boat and use it regularly

- My children will be happy, healthy and successful

- I will travel to at least one new country each year

Three-year objectives:

- I will have a portfolio generating a minimum of £100k leveraged income

- I will have written a book

- I will have bought a property for my father

- I will have run a marathon

- I will have built a solar-powered summerhouse/ office/library in the garden

Twelve-month goals:

- I will have a leveraged income of £50k per annum from property
- I will spend a minimum of two hours per day and four hours a day at weekends with my children
- I will only work one evening per week after 7pm and spend time with my wife and children on the other evenings
- I will have a minimum of four one-week holidays abroad with my family
- I will take tennis coaching once a week

Three-month goals:

- I will buy one more HMO property
- I will take time off to plan my goals with my wife
- I will try a new diet
- I will take my kids away for a long weekend on their own

One of the primary goals I would encourage for the majority of people is getting to the point where your monthly leveraged income exceeds your expenses. The day that happens – which I call 'financial independence day' – it's a huge weight off your mind, knowing you don't have to get up every morning and go out to work to pay the bills. Attaining that first level of financial independence and replacing your salary-based income with property income should be an eighteen to thirty-six month plan. If you want some inspiration, go back and take another look at Bill Mann's story.

Remember to make your goals visual. Vision boards are great for focusing on the bigger picture, but where you have specific, measurable goals and targets, a simple line graph will show whether you're on target for achieving what you want in the timeframe you want it. Mark your X and Y axis values out, then draw a line from the origin to the top right-hand corner: the goal end value. For example, if your leveraged income is £2,000 a month and you set yourself a goal of increasing it to £4,000 a month within a year, your line graph might look like this:

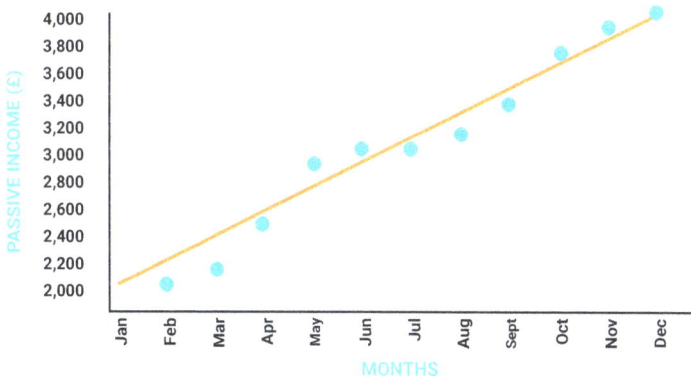

Fig 12.1: Set a goal for your income over time

Each month when you mark on the amount of your leveraged income, it wants to be as close to the line as possible. If it's above it, you're likely to exceed your goal. Put the graph up somewhere you'll keep seeing it, and tell the rest of your family (and your mentor or coach) what you're doing. The more people who know you've set yourself goals, the more likely you are to achieve them.

As your business grows, your goals will change – what you set down today for the next five years is not set in stone, because the more you achieve, the more you will believe is possible.

Preparation is one of the keys to success in any business, and that includes preparing yourself mentally and practically for the 'back of house' activity that's going to keep the engines running. If you're planning to build a portfolio rather than just make a one-off investment, don't underestimate how much time you'll need to dedicate to administering your business, particularly when you get involved with refurbishment and renting out properties. You need to be able to hit the ground running. That means being computer literate and familiar with certain basic business practices and terminology, all of which will help you achieve and measure success. If you do have gaps in your skills, then find others who can support you.

Remember, you can spend your life looking for the perfect deal, but it's enough just to find a good one. Provided you've put in the time and effort with your preparation and due diligence, you should be able to make a worthwhile investment, and you can work on refining your technique and getting better deals as you go on.

A final checklist

- You've got a written list of goals and objectives

- You've looked at the different investment options out there and decided on the one(s) that fit your financial capital and return requirements

- You've spent time talking to other successful investors and have identified some mentors or organisations/professional advisors you're confident can help you move forward

- You've reviewed and expanded your network

- You've done your due diligence on property companies and/or markets offering opportunities

- You know the top mistakes that people make, and how you can avoid them

- Your administration systems and professional services support network are in place

- You've stood and continue to stand on the

shoulders of giants and develop relationships
with people

- You have a plan for continually investing in
yourself

And remember, as you go through your property investment journey, to always surround yourself with the best people who will keep raising you up. There will be times when it gets hard, when all your capital seems to be tied up, not every deal will go to plan, and you'll undoubtedly experience 'the dip', but don't be tempted to give up. Follow what successful people are doing, be the person you want to be and never stop learning.

I sincerely hope you've enjoyed this book and I would like to wish you the very best of success. I'm passionate about helping people to *be* more, *do* more, *have* more and *give* more in life, and one of the ways that I do that is through books, social media and podcasts, so please feel free to connect with me and my communities of likeminded and high-net-worth individuals at www.stevebolton.com

Join my online partner network to connect with me directly and receive free virtual mentoring:
www.facebook.com/stevebolton99/

Find free resources and tools:
https://platinumpropertypartners.co.uk/free-resources

Acknowledgements

A huge thanks to Charlotte Flake, Amy Grohmann and the amazing staff and partners at Platinum, Bourne, Bolt and team CHX, without whom this book would not have been possible.

The Author

Steve is the Founder of Platinum Property Partners which, through its franchise network, has purchased more than £300 million of property and created more than 6,000 affordable new rental homes.

Steve Bolton left school at sixteen with no qualifications, but went on to start multiple businesses with seven- and eight-figure valuations. Through his businesses he has either directly or indirectly mentored and inspired more than 100,000 people.

He also owns stakes in businesses in the fields of residential and commercial property, franchising, marketing, mentoring and tech.

Steve is a very active philanthropist, with a long-term goal to help end homelessness in Britain and has also committed in his will to give away 51% of his wealth to good causes.

Steve is a father of four, a boat and water lover and, since 2004, he has taken three months' holiday every year to travel the world and spend quality time with his family.

To contact Steve:

Website: https://stevebolton.com
LinkedIn: www.linkedin.com/in/steveboltonppp
Twitter: @steve_bolton
Facebook: www.facebook.com/stevebolton99

.

www.ingramcontent.com/pod-product-compliance
Lightning Source LLC
Chambersburg PA
CBHW070349200326
41518CB00012B/2180